The
PRESSURE COOKER
Cookbook

The
PRESSURE COOKER
Cookbook

by
Toula Patsalis

Illustrations by
Michelle Burchard

HPBooks

HPBooks
are published by
The Berkley Publishing Group
A member of Penguin Putnam Inc.
375 Hudson Street
New York, NY 10014

The Penguin Putnam Inc. World Wide Web site address is
http://www.penguinputnam.com

Library of Congress Cataloging-in-Publication Data

Patsalis, Toula.
The pressure cooker cookbook.—1st HPBooks ed.
            p.   cm.
    ISBN 1-55788-189-8 (acid-free paper)
    1. Pressure cookery.   I. Title.
        TX840.P7P34   1994
    641.5'87—dc20   94-19241
                              CIP

Cover photograph © 1994 by Cormier Photography
Printed in the United States of America
13   14   15   16   17   18   19   20   21

Acknowledgments

First and foremost, my heartfelt thanks to my husband, Chris, for his confidence and encouragement to complete this book, and to my children, Harry and Julie, my taste-testers, for their unconditional love of my recipes.

Gratefully and lovingly this book is dedicated to those who have taught me to enjoy the many delicious wonders of food preparation.

To my mother, who introduced me to the healthy flavors of our Greek heritage.

To my father, who instilled the fine delicate flavors of quality.

To the many food mentors and instructors who helped orchestrate my knowledge of methods and techniques: Julia Child, Jacques Pepin, Nick Malgiere, Lynne Kasper, Marlene Sorosky, Cleo Gruber, Jane Schermehorn, and Guilda Krause, to name only a few.

Contents

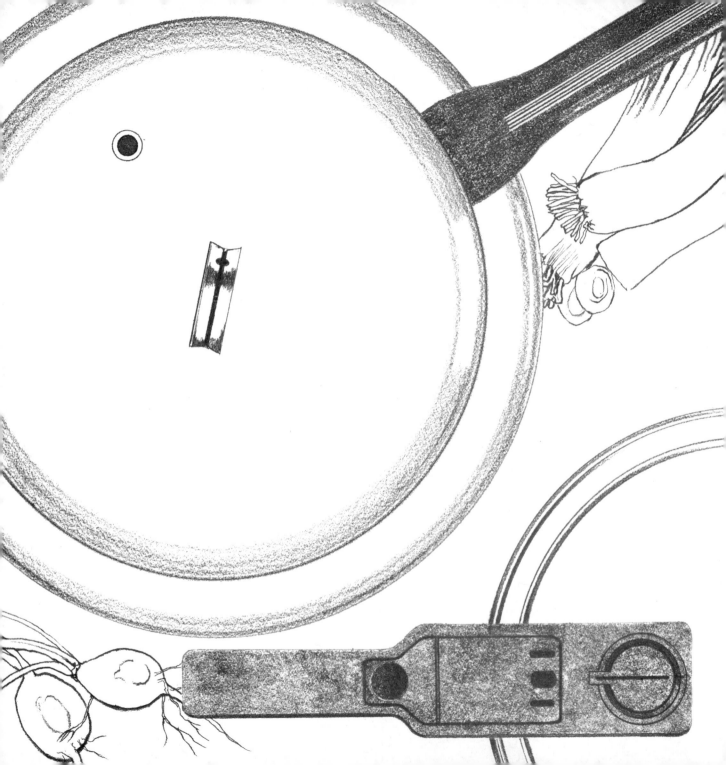

Introduction

Pressure cooking has certainly added a new dimension to my culinary life! I have discovered that the pressure cooker is a marvelous kitchen tool that can be conveniently used for speedy meal preparation, producing nutritious, mouthwatering dishes with enhanced flavors and vibrant eye appeal. In addition to saving time, a pressure cooker also saves energy. Yes, pressure cooking is perfect for today's active lifestyles. Within these pages, I offer you tested and retested recipes that will soon become your favorites.

As you leaf through the chapters, you will be inspired by the shortcuts that can be accomplished in planning menus for entertaining and cooking for everyday meals. Timesaving appetizers filled with flavors of many countries will surely be a hit with family and guests. The soups and stews are filled with fresh and healthy ingredients, perfectly balanced with fresh herbs and spices. It will soon become apparent that leaner, less expensive cuts of meats can be cooked tender and succulent in minutes. Fish and shellfish dishes will be cooked to perfection when you follow the easy instructions. And the dessert chapter, filled with creamy cheesecakes, lemon curd, chocolate pudding, bread puddings, and sauces, is not to be missed. There are jams and chutneys to be enjoyed at home or given as gifts.

Pressure cooking is uniquely different. The methods, techniques, and timing are altered from conventional cooking. In some recipes, cooking time is reduced by 70 percent. Once the steps for converting standard conventional recipes to pressure cooking are followed and learned, you will find a new culinary world of convenience and ease that will encourage you to become more adventurous.

Yes, I am a pressure cooking convert! Unlike those pressure cookers of the 1940s, the new technology is safer. I am intrigued by the science and technology behind these wonderful units and astonished at the marvelous results. The testing and development of the recipes was a lengthy procedure and one idea led to another. I felt an urge to push the pressure cooker to its limits, only to find that its boundaries were endless.

While testing and developing these recipes, I became a pressure cooking addict! Although I have not come to the point of giving up my quality skillets, saucepans, or microwave oven, I truly feel the pressure cooker is a fine tool that should be in every kitchen next to the finest kitchen tools and equipment. The pressure cooker can make it possible for all of us to cook and enjoy good, healthy meals. This hassle-free method of food preparation will be your right hand, whether preparing casual snacks, fabulous meals, or beautiful foods for entertaining.

Hopefully, you will come to enjoy the ease and convenience of pressure cooking. The recipes are designed to be followed step by step, leading to wonderful results. Overcome your fear and use your pressure cooker frequently. Soon it will prove itself in value and you will find yourself reaching for it every day.

I can't remember having more fun and feeling more enthusiasm about a cooking method during my many years involved in food preparation. Now I invite you to share the pleasure and flavors of the adventure of pressure cooking.

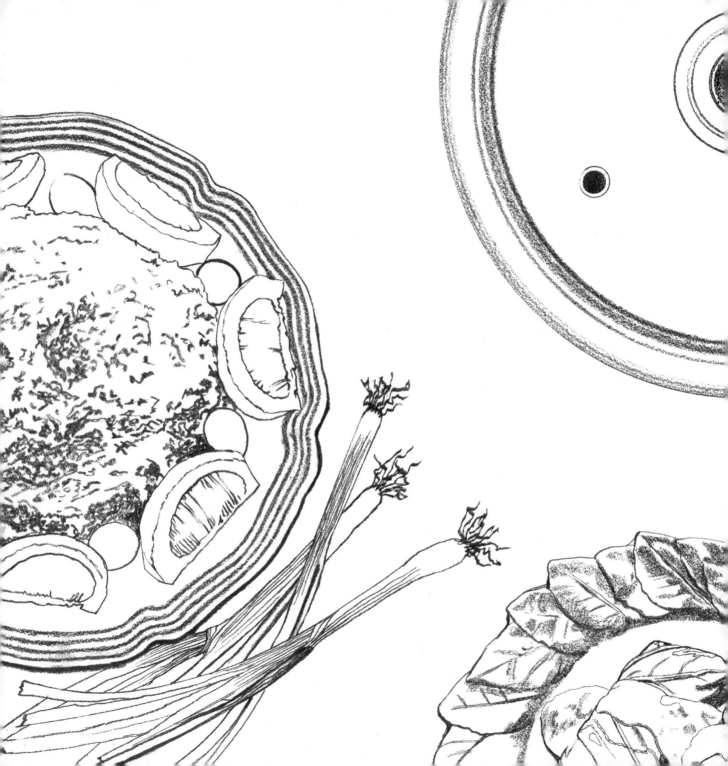

Appetizers

Great beginnings for any festive get-together, appetizers and hors d'oeuvres are always a welcome sight for hungry guests. Set the mood with a welcoming display. Many of the recipes in this chapter can be made ahead and frozen.

Plan a balance of cocktail hors d'oeuvres for a stand-up party. Try to have at least eight servings of cocktail hors d'oeuvre per person. The variety should include fresh vegetables and fruit pieces for dieters. Be prepared to refill platters throughout the party.

If you are planning appetizers for a dinner party, keep it light. One hot and one cold appetizer is plenty before you invite your guests to sit down for dinner.

Include bowls of munchies such as a mixture of nuts or seasoned popcorn and position the bowls around the entertainment area.

Black Bean Appetizer with Sour Cream, Chopped Tomato, & Avocado Slices

Cilantro resembles flat-leaf parsley. If you're not sure which is which, pinch off a leaf and smell to make sure it isn't parsley.

1/2 cup dried black beans
2 cups water
3 slices bacon, cut in 1/2-inch pieces
1 small onion, minced
2 garlic cloves, crushed
1 1/2 cups beef broth
1 1/4 teaspoons salt
1 1/2 teaspoons chili powder

1/2 teaspoon red pepper flakes
1/4 teaspoon ground cumin
1/3 cup chopped cilantro
1 tablespoon sherry
1 large tomato
1 ripe avocado
1 (8-oz.) carton sour cream

Place beans in a bowl, add water to the beans, and soak 4 hours.

In a pressure cooker, sauté bacon, stirring until crisp. Add onion and garlic; cook 2 additional minutes, stirring often. Add broth, salt, chili powder, pepper flakes, cumin, cilantro, sherry, and beans, mixing well. Secure lid. Over high heat, develop steam to high pressure. Reduce heat to maintain pressure and cook 10 minutes.

Release pressure according to manufacturer's directions. Remove the lid. Drain beans through a sieve.

Beans may be served hot or chilled. Cooked beans can be refrigerated up to 2 days or frozen up to 1 month.

Seed and coarsely chop tomato. Cut avocado in half, remove pit, peel, and cut into slices. To serve, mound about 3 tablespoons beans on a small dish. Top with dollop of sour cream, spoon several chunks tomato over sour cream, and garnish with avocado slice. Repeat with remaining ingredients. Makes 6 to 8 servings.

Baba Ghanouhi (Middle Eastern Eggplant Dip)

To ensure that the eggplant is ripe, look for a well-rounded bottom without a deep dimple at the base. The skin should be smooth and unblemished.

1 large eggplant (1 1/2 pounds)
1 cup water
1 teaspoon salt
1/2 teaspoon pepper
1/3 cup fresh lemon juice

1/3 cup tahini (sesame seed paste)
2 garlic cloves
2 slices bread, crusts trimmed and crumbled
Pita bread or toast points

Lay eggplant on its side. Cut a 2-inch-thick slice from top of eggplant horizontally. Using a grapefruit knife or a large tablespoon, remove pulp from eggplant, leaving a 1-inch-thick shell. Reserve shell. Place the pulp in steam basket of pressure cooker.

Pour water into pressure cooker and insert the steam basket. Sprinkle eggplant pulp with salt and pepper. Secure lid. Over high heat, develop steam to high pressure. Reduce heat to maintain pressure and cook 3 minutes.

Release pressure according to manufacturer's directions. Remove lid. Lift steam basket from the pressure cooker and drain off excess water.

Place eggplant pulp in a food processor or blender. Add lemon juice, tahini, garlic, and bread. Process until almost smooth. Spoon mixture into eggplant shell. Serve with pieces of pita bread cut into triangles or toast points. Makes 12 servings.

Cook's Note: Dip does not freeze well.

Honey Sesame Chicken Wing Appetizer

The honey adds sweetness, aids in browning, and helps the flavorings cling to the chicken.

2 tablespoons olive oil
2 tablespoons sesame oil
12 chicken wings, cut apart at joints
1/2 cup chicken broth
1/2 cup plus 2 tablespoons honey, divided
1/4 cup soy sauce

2 tablespoons sherry
2 garlic cloves, crushed
1 teaspoon crushed red pepper flakes
3/4 teaspoon grated ginger root or 1/4 teaspoon ground ginger
1/4 cup sesame seeds

In a pressure cooker, heat oils, add chicken, and sauté, turning to brown on all sides. Using tongs, remove chicken and set aside. Combine broth, 1/2 cup honey, soy sauce, sherry, garlic, pepper flakes, and ginger root in pressure cooker; stir well. Place chicken wings in sauce and gently mix to coat. Secure lid. Over high heat, develop steam to medium-high pressure. Reduce heat to maintain pressure and cook 3 minutes.

Release pressure according to manufacturer's directions. Remove lid. Stir chicken and sauce.

Preheat broiler. Place chicken wings on broiler pan. Combine 1/4 of sauce, sesame seeds, and remaining honey. Brush mixture over chicken wings. Broil until golden on one side, turn, brush with sauce, and broil other side until golden.

Serve hot or cold. Makes 8 servings.

Cook's Note: Chicken wings may be frozen up to 1 month before serving. Thaw in refrigerator before broiling.

Chicken Pinwheel Appetizer

These pinwheels are bursting with flavor and have great eye appeal.

4 chicken breast halves, skin removed and
  boned
1/2 pound Italian sweet sausage, casing
  removed
1/4 green bell pepper, minced
2 green onions, minced
1 garlic clove, minced
2 slices bread, crumbled

1 tablespoon butter
1/3 cup parsley leaves, minced
1 egg
1 cup water
Bread rounds or crackers
Berry preserves

Using a meat mallet, gently flatten chicken breasts between two pieces of waxed paper to 1/8 inch thickness, being careful not to shred meat.

In a bowl, combine sausage, bell pepper, green onions, garlic, bread crumbs, butter, parsley, and egg. Mix, then knead 1 minute. Spread about 1/4 cup of sausage mixture on each chicken piece. Roll up, ending with seam side down. Enclose with plastic wrap, lightly twisting ends to secure. Place rolls in steam basket. Pour water into pressure cooker and insert steam basket. Secure lid. Over high heat, develop steam to medium-high pressure. Reduce heat to maintain pressure and cook 8 minutes.

Release pressure according to manufacturer's directions. Remove lid. Lift steam basket from pressure cooker and transfer rolls to a wire rack. Cool 1 hour.

Remove plastic wrap from rolls and cut into 1/2-inch slices. Serve on round, sliced bread. Garnish with 1/2 teaspoon preserves.

Chicken rolls, cooked or uncooked, may be frozen up to 2 months. Makes about 30 slices.

Cook's Note: To make bread rounds, trim crust from bread. Use a 2 1/2-inch round cookie cutter and press out rounds. Toast on a baking sheet 8 minutes in a preheated 375°F (190°C) oven. Wrap in plastic wrap to keep fresh.

Layered Tortilla Dip

Enough to feed a crowd, the pressure cooker helps put this together quickly.

Meat Sauce with Beans (see opposite)
Guacamole (see opposite)
1 (14- or 15-oz.) package tortilla chips
1/2 head iceberg lettuce, shredded
2 cups (8 ounces) shredded Monterey Jack
  cheese, divided
3 tomatoes, seeds removed and chopped
6 green onions, chopped
1 green bell pepper, chopped
1 cup pitted ripe olives, cut in halves

Meat Sauce with Beans:

1 cup dried kidney beans
1/4 cup olive oil
1 large onion, chopped
2 garlic cloves, crushed
1 pound ground beef or ground turkey
1 (8-oz.) can tomato sauce
1 cup beef broth
1 tablespoon brown sugar
1 teaspoon salt
2 teaspoons chili powder
1 teaspoon each crushed red pepper flakes
  and ground cumin

Guacamole:

2 ripe avocados, peeled and pits removed
2 tablespoons fresh lemon juice
2 garlic cloves, crushed
3 green onions, cut into pieces
3 tablespoons salsa
2 tablespoons olive oil
1/3 cup sour cream
1/2 teaspoon salt

Prepare Meat Sauce with Beans. While mixture cooks, prepare Guacamole.
  Place chips in center of 14- to 16-inch round platter or pizza pan, leaving 2-inch wide space around edge. Arrange lettuce around edge of platter. Sprinkle half of cheese over chips. Spoon meat sauce over cheese. Scatter tomatoes, green onions, bell pepper, and olives over meat layer. Sprinkle with remaining cheese. Place spoonfuls of Guacamole over cheese. Makes 16 servings.

Meat Sauce with Beans

Soak beans in 4 cups water at least 4 hours. Drain and set aside.

In a pressure cooker, heat oil. Add onion and garlic and sauté until softened. Add beef to onion mixture and cook, stirring to break up meat, until no longer pink. Add drained beans, tomato sauce, broth, brown sugar, salt, chili powder, pepper flakes, and cumin; mix well. Secure lid. Over high heat, develop steam to high pressure. Reduce heat to maintain pressure and cook 10 minutes.

Release pressure according to manufacturer's directions. Remove lid. Set aside.

Guacamole

Combine all ingredients in a food processor. Process until smooth. Cover surface with plastic wrap.

Cook's Note: Prepared meat sauce may be frozen up to 3 months. Thaw overnight in the refrigerator before reheating. The sauce is also great for Coney Island hot dogs.

Hummus (Chickpea Spread)

The flavor of the dried chickpea, or garbanzo bean, is sweeter and nuttier than the canned ones.

1 cup dried chickpeas
2 cups water
3 sprigs parsley
1 teaspoon dried spearmint, rubbed between palms
1 teaspoon salt
1/4 teaspoon pepper

2 garlic cloves, crushed
1/3 cup olive oil
1/4 cup lemon juice
2 teaspoons tahini (sesame seed paste)
1/2 cup yogurt
Pita bread wedges or toast points to serve

Place chickpeas in a bowl, add water to come 2 inches above chickpeas, and soak 4 to 6 hours. Drain.

In a pressure cooker, combine drained chickpeas, the 2 cups water, parsley, spearmint, salt, and pepper. Secure lid. Over high heat, develop steam to high pressure. Reduce heat to maintain pressure and cook 15 minutes.

Release pressure according to manufacturer's directions. Remove lid. Drain chickpeas through a colander. Remove parsley sprigs. Combine chickpeas, garlic, oil, lemon juice, tahini, and yogurt in a food processor or blender. Blend until smooth.

Serve spread with pita bread wedges or toast points. Makes 6 servings.

Mexichicken Tacos

Always a winner, these tacos are a real treat for football Sundays!

2 tablespoons olive oil
3 slices bacon, cut into 1/2-inch pieces
1 medium-size onion, sliced
3 garlic cloves, crushed
1/3 cup cilantro, finely chopped
1/3 cup jalapeño salsa
1/4 cup ketchup
1/2 cup chicken broth
1 teaspoon salt
1 teaspoon chili powder
2 chicken breasts, skin removed, boned, and
   cut into 2-inch strips

1/3 cup sour cream
1 tablespoon potato starch or flour
1 (24-count) package miniature taco shells
1 cup (4 ounces) shredded Monterey Jack
   cheese
2 cups shredded lettuce
1 green bell pepper, coarsely chopped
1 large tomato, seeds removed and coarsely
   chopped
2 avocados, thinly sliced

In a pressure cooker, heat oil. Add bacon; sauté 1 minute. Add onion, garlic, and cilantro; sauté 3 minutes. Stir in salsa, ketchup, broth, salt, chili powder, and chicken strips. Secure lid. Over high heat, develop steam to medium pressure. Reduce to maintain pressure and cook 5 minutes.

Release pressure according to manufacturer's directions. Remove lid. Stir chicken and sauce.

Combine sour cream and potato starch. Stir into chicken and sauce and cook, stirring, over medium heat 1 minute or until mixture thickens.

Place taco shells on a large tray. Spoon chicken and sauce into shells. Add a little cheese, lettuce, bell pepper, and tomato to each filled shell, topping with sliced avocado.

Chicken filling may be frozen up to 3 months. Thaw in refrigerator overnight before reheating. Makes 24 servings.

Cook's Note: Potato starch is a thickener that also adds flavor to recipes.

Salmon Mousse

It makes a lovely presentation to mold the mousse in a fish-shaped mold. Invert onto a platter. Unmold by wrapping hot towels around bottom of mold. Cut a cucumber into very thin slices and use the slices to cover the fish in rows resembling the scales of a fish. Use pimento-stuffed olives for eyes.

1 envelope unflavored gelatin
1/3 cup lemon juice
1/4 cup butter or olive oil
3 shallots, minced
1 cup bottled clam juice
1 bay leaf
1 teaspoon salt
1/4 teaspoon white pepper

1 teaspoon dill weed
1 pound salmon steaks, 1 inch thick
1 tablespoon sherry
1/2 cup sour cream
1/2 cup mayonnaise
Lemon slices to garnish
Dark bread or crackers

Soften gelatin in lemon juice in a small bowl and set aside. In a pressure cooker, melt butter. Add shallots and sauté over medium heat until softened. Stir in clam juice, bay leaf, salt, pepper, and dill, mixing well. Place salmon steaks in clam liquid. Secure lid. Over high heat, develop steam to medium-high pressure. Reduce heat to maintain pressure and cook 3 minutes.

Release pressure according to manufacturer's directions. Remove lid.

Place salmon steaks on a platter, reserving cooking liquid. Remove bay leaf. Remove skin and bones from salmon and discard.

Combine salmon, cooking liquid, dissolved gelatin, sherry, sour cream, and mayonnaise in a food processor or blender. Blend until smooth. Pour into a 6-cup mold or serving bowl. Refrigerate, covered with plastic wrap, overnight or at least 6 hours. Unmold on a serving plate if desired.

Garnish with lemon slices and serve with hearty dark bread, cut into triangles, or crackers. Makes 16 servings.

Cook's Note: Salmon Mousse can be made up to 2 days ahead.

Pickled Beets

Pickled beets add a dark, ruby-red garnish to salad and cold dishes.

4 large (3-inch) beets, cut in half
1 onion, sliced
3 garlic cloves, crushed
1/2 cup white wine vinegar

1/2 cup sugar
3/4 teaspoon salt
2 teaspoons crushed caraway seeds
1/4 cup olive oil

Combine beets, onion, garlic, vinegar, sugar, salt, caraway seeds, and oil in a pressure cooker. Secure lid. Over high heat, develop steam to high pressure. Reduce heat to maintain pressure and cook 10 minutes. Release pressure according to manufacturer's directions. Remove lid.

Using tongs, transfer beets to a bowl of ice water; reserve cooking juices in pressure cooker.

Gently rub beets to remove skin. Cut beets horizontally into 1/4-inch slices. Place in a deep bowl. Strain cooking juices over beets. Refrigerate, lightly covered, at least 2 hours before serving. Makes 6 servings.

Cook's Note: Drain beets and serve as appetizer or salad topping. Do not freeze. The beets in cooking liquid can be refrigerated up to 2 weeks.

Stuffed Grape Leaves

Make these ahead and serve as part of an appetizer tray.

---

1 (16-oz.) jar grape leaves
1/3 cup olive oil
4 green onions, minced
3 garlic cloves, crushed
1/3 cup fresh parsley, minced
1/3 cup fresh mint, minced, or 2 teaspoons
   dried mint leaves
1 cup rice

2 cups chicken broth
1 1/2 teaspoons salt, divided
1/4 teaspoon pepper
1/2 teaspoon grated lemon zest
2 cups water
1/2 cup fresh lemon juice

Drain grape leaves and rinse well in warm water. In a pressure cooker, heat oil. Add green onions, garlic, parsley, and mint and sauté in hot oil 2 minutes. Stir in rice and cook, stirring, 1 minute. Stir in broth, 1 teaspoon salt, pepper, and lemon zest, mixing thoroughly. Secure lid. Over high heat, develop steam to high pressure. Reduce heat to maintain pressure and cook 8 minutes. Release pressure according to manufacturer's directions. Remove lid. Transfer rice mixture to a bowl. Rinse pressure cooker.

Place grape leaves, rib side up, in a row on work surface. Trim thick rib from bottom of each leaf. Spoon 2 teaspoons of rice filling on each leaf. Fold sides of leaf to center of filling, then roll from bottom to top. Place in steam basket seam side down. (Extra grape leaves may be tightly wrapped in plastic wrap and frozen.) Pour the water and remaining 1/2 teaspoon salt into pressure cooker. Insert steam basket with grape leaves. Pour lemon juice over stuffed grape leaves. Cover leaves with heavy plastic wrap, pressing around edges. Secure lid. Over high heat, develop steam to high pressure. Reduce heat to maintain pressure and cook 10 minutes.

Release pressure according to manufacturer's directions. Remove lid.

Remove steam basket and let stand, covered, 5 minutes. Serve stuffed grape leaves hot or cold. Makes 16 servings.

Cook's Note: Refrigerate stuffed grape leaves in an airtight container up to 2 days. Also, they may be frozen up to 3 months; thaw in refrigerator before serving.

Scandinavian Meatballs in Gravy

Serve meatballs in a chafing dish as an appetizer or with buttered noodles as a main course.

1/2 pound ground beef
1/2 pound ground pork sausage
2 slices bread, crumbled
1 egg
1 small onion, minced
1 garlic clove, crushed
1 teaspoons salt, divided
1/2 teaspoon pepper, divided

1/2 cup butter
1 medium-size onion, diced
1 1/2 cups beef broth
1 tablespoon tomato paste
1 bay leaf
1/3 cup sour cream
1 tablespoon potato starch or flour

Combine beef, sausage, bread, egg, minced onion, garlic, 1/2 teaspoon salt, and 1/4 teaspoon pepper in a bowl. Mix with your hand 1 minute or until combined. Shape mixture into 1 1/2-inch meatballs. Set aside.

In a pressure cooker, melt butter. Add onion and sauté in butter over medium heat 2 minutes. Add meatballs, broth, tomato paste, bay leaf, and remaining 1/2 teaspoon salt and 1/4 teaspoon pepper. Secure lid. Over high heat, develop steam to medium-high pressure. Reduce heat to maintain pressure and cook 5 minutes. Release pressure according to manufacturer's directions. Remove lid.

Combine sour cream and potato starch in a small bowl. Stir into meatball mixture. Cook, stirring, over medium-high heat 1 minute or until sauce thickens. Makes 16 appetizer servings.

Variation

One pound of ground turkey breast may be substituted for the beef and sausage.

Cook's Note: Meatballs with sauce may be frozen up to 3 months.

Stuffed Red-Skinned Potatoes with Caviar

Make these easy caviar-topped appetizers ahead for your next party.

---

10 small (2-inch-diameter) red-skinned potatoes,
  rinsed
2 cups water
1/3 cup sour cream

1 teaspoon salt
1 green onion, minced
1 tablespoon grated Parmesan cheese
1 small jar golden or black caviar

Pierce each potato once with a cake tester or skewer.

Pour the water into a pressure cooker. Layer potatoes in steam basket and place basket in pressure cooker. Secure lid. Over high heat, develop steam to medium-high pressure. Reduce heat to maintain pressure and cook 10 minutes. Release pressure according to manufacturer's directions. Remove lid. Remove steam basket and place potatoes in basket under cold, running water 1 minute. Drain well.

With a sharp knife, cut potatoes in half. Using melon baller or small teaspoon, scoop out potato pulp, leaving thin shell. Set shells aside.

Mash potato pulp with a fork until nearly smooth. Add sour cream, salt, green onion, and cheese; blend well. Spoon potato mixture into shells, topping each with dollop of caviar. Refrigerate, covered, until served. Makes 20 servings.

Variation

Use sautéed crisp bacon pieces as a topping instead of caviar.

Cook's Note: Stuffed potatoes may be frozen up to 3 months. Thaw in refrigerator before serving.

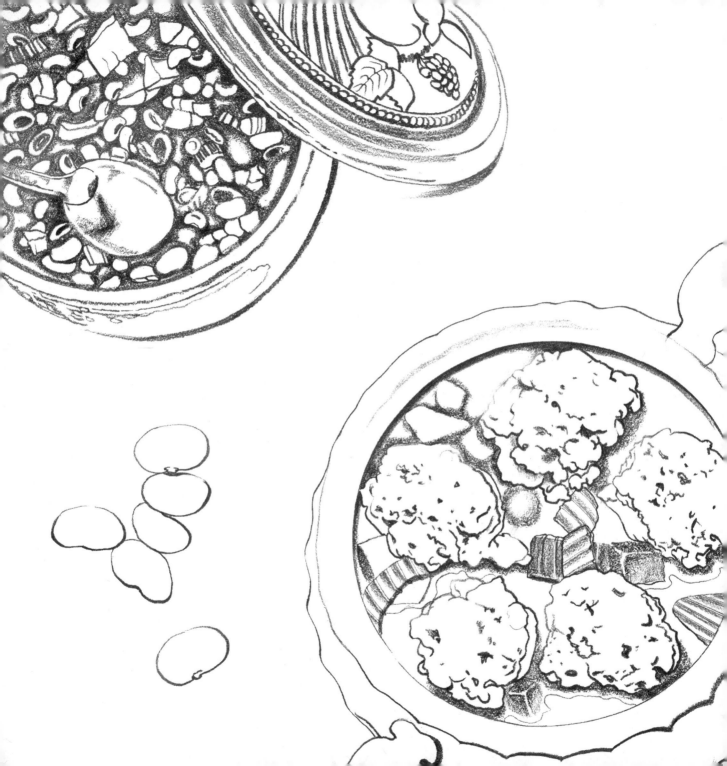

Soups

The basis for a hearty, rich soup is a good stock. The pressure cooker quickly and easily extracts all the flavors and nutrients from bones and vegetables.

Several stock recipes are offered in this chapter. They are all moderately seasoned and offer a well-balanced base for soups or stews. However, if a canned stock is preferred, select one with a low sodium content.

Favorite soup recipes are easily adapted to pressure cooking. Begin with a good stock, keeping in mind that because very little evaporation occurs during cooking, the liquid should be decreased by a cup. Begin with ingredients that require longer periods to cook and interrupt the process (see Eight Steps for Perfect Pressure Cooking on page 188) to add ingredients that require less time. Refer to time charts for guidance.

Vegetable Stock

This low-fat, flavorful stock may be substituted for any poultry, meat, or fish stock.
Vegetables may be used with peels.

3 tablespoons olive oil or canola oil
3 large leeks, coarsely chopped
2 garlic cloves, crushed
1/2 cup parsley, minced
2 tablespoons all-purpose flour
4 carrots, cut into 1-inch pieces
6 celery stalks with leaves, cut into 1-inch pieces
10 cups water
1/4 cup fresh lemon juice
2 large zucchini, cut into 3-inch chunks

1 (10-oz.) package fresh spinach, rinsed twice in warm water
1 large sweet potato with peel, cut into 1-inch cubes
2 bay leaves
1/2 teaspoon dried tarragon
1 teaspoon dried thyme
3/4 teaspoon ground fennel
2 teaspoons salt
1/2 teaspoon white pepper

In a pressure cooker, heat oil. Add leeks, garlic, and parsley and sauté in hot oil over medium-high heat. With a wooden spoon, stir in flour and cook 3 minutes. Add carrots, celery, water, and lemon juice. Stir well, scraping particles from the bottom of the pressure cooker. Add remaining ingredients and stir well. Secure lid and increase heat to high. Develop pressure to high. Reduce heat to maintain pressure. Cook 20 minutes.

Release pressure according to manufacturer's directions. Remove lid. Strain stock into a 5-quart saucepan and return to high heat. Boil 10 minutes. Makes 2 quarts.

Cook's Note: You may use stock immediately in your favorite soup recipe, store in refrigerator up to 2 days, or freeze in airtight containers up to 2 months. Thaw in refrigerator.

Chicken or Turkey Stock

Stock may be reduced for sauces by boiling over medium-high heat 10 minutes. Flavors will intensify.

3 pounds chicken or turkey pieces (wings, necks, and bones)
2 large leeks, sliced
2 garlic cloves
1 carrot, cut into large chunks
2 celery stalks, cut into 2-inch pieces
2 teaspoons salt

1/2 teaspoon white pepper
1 bay leaf
2 tablespoons bouquet garni in a cheesecloth bag (see page 191)
3 parsley sprigs
3 quarts water

In a 6-quart pressure cooker, combine chicken, leeks, garlic, carrot, celery, salt, pepper, bay leaf, bouquet garni, parsley, and water. Secure lid. Over high heat, develop steam to high pressure. Reduce heat to maintain pressure and cook 1 hour. Release pressure according to manufacturer's directions. Shake cooker to release pressure pockets. Remove lid.

Stir stock. Remove cheesecloth bag, bay leaf, and chicken pieces. Strain stock through a fine colander, sieve, or cheesecloth into large pot or container, lightly pressing with back of large spoon to extract juices from vegetables.

Refrigerate a few hours, allowing fat to rise to top of stock for easy removal. Makes 2 1/2 quarts.

Cook's Note: You may use stock immediately in your favorite soup recipe, store in refrigerator up to 3 days, or freeze in airtight containers up to 2 months. Thaw in refrigerator.

Basic Beef Stock

Make your own stock and forget the canned ones. This is so much better!

1/4 cup olive oil
2 carrots, cut into 1/4-inch cubes
2 celery stalks, cut into 1/4-inch slices
2 medium-size onions, chopped
3 pounds meaty beef bones, split by butcher
1 cup dry white wine
3 garlic cloves, mashed
1 teaspoon dried thyme

1/2 teaspoon dried tarragon
2 bay leaves
3 large parsley sprigs
1 teaspoon peppercorns, freshly ground
2 teaspoons salt or to taste
1 teaspoon brown sugar
10 cups water

Preheat oven to 425°F (220°C). Combine oil, carrots, celery, and onions in a baking pan, stirring to thoroughly coat vegetables with oil. Add beef bones. Bake, stirring frequently, 35 minutes or until vegetables and bones are a deep, golden brown.

Transfer vegetables and bones into a pressure cooker.

Place baking pan over medium heat and add wine. Scrape to dislodge caramelized cooking juices clinging to bottom of pan. Add wine mixture to pressure cooker, along with garlic, herbs, peppercorns, salt, brown sugar, and the water. Secure lid. Over high heat, develop steam to high pressure. Reduce heat to maintain pressure and cook 1 hour. Release pressure according to manufacturer's directions. Shake well. Remove lid and stir vegetable-bone mixture.

Using a slotted spoon, remove bones and set aside. Strain stock through a fine sieve into a 4-quart pan. Using back of large spoon, press vegetable pulp through sieve into stock. Remove meat from bones and add to stock. Boil stock 8 minutes. Makes 2 quarts.

Variation

Veal bones may be substituted for beef to make veal stock.

Cook's Note: You may use stock immediately in your favorite soup recipe, store in refrigerator up to 3 days, or freeze in airtight containers up to 3 months. Thaw in refrigerator.

Rich Fish Stock

This mild fish stock is prepared quickly and is filled with flavor.

1/3 cup olive oil
2 medium-size leeks, thickly sliced
2 garlic cloves, unpeeled and quartered
1 large carrot, cut into 2-inch pieces
2 celery stalks, cut into 2-inch pieces
6 sprigs parsley
1 1/2 pounds fish heads, tails, and bones
   (available from fish monger)

1 (8-oz.) bottle clam juice
2 cups white wine
4 cups water
1 tablespoon fresh lemon juice
1 teaspoon salt
1/4 teaspoon white pepper
2 tablespoons bouquet garni in cheesecloth
   bag (see page 191)

In a pressure cooker, heat oil. Add leeks, garlic, carrot, celery, and parsley and sauté in hot oil 3 minutes, stirring occasionally. Stir in fish pieces, clam juice, wine, water, lemon juice, salt, pepper, and bouquet garni. Secure lid. Over high heat, develop steam to medium-high pressure. Reduce heat to maintain pressure and cook 10 minutes. Release pressure according to manufacturer's directions. Remove lid.

Strain stock through a cheesecloth-lined colander into a large bowl. Using back of large spoon, press vegetables and fish pieces to extract juices.

Use stock immediately in your favorite soup recipe, store in refrigerator up to 3 days, or freeze in airtight container up to 3 months. Thaw in refrigerator. Makes 1 ½ quarts.

Cook's Note: Fish stock becomes bitter if overcooked.

Black-Eyed Pea & Sausage Soup

Serve soup with chunks of hard-crusted bread.

2 cups (12 ounces) dried black-eyed peas
1/2 pound bacon, cut into 1/2-inch pieces
1 large red onion, minced
3 garlic cloves, chopped
6 cups canned or fresh chicken broth
1/4 cup tomato paste
2 teaspoons dried Greek oregano
1 bay leaf

1 teaspoon coarse sea salt or granulated salt
1 teaspoon crushed red pepper flakes
3 tablespoons brown sugar
1/2 pound turkey kielbasa, cut into 1-inch
  pieces
1/3 cup chopped green bell pepper
1/3 cup parsley, chopped coarsely

Sort dried peas and remove any foreign particles. Place in a large strainer and rinse under warm, running water, tossing to thoroughly clean peas. Transfer to a bowl and add water to measure 2 inches above peas. Let soak at least 4 hours. Drain peas and set aside.

In a pressure cooker, sauté bacon until crisp. Add onion and garlic and cook until onion is softened, about 3 minutes. Add peas to bacon mixture and stir well. Add broth, tomato paste, oregano, bay leaf, salt, pepper flakes, and brown sugar. Stir until thoroughly mixed. Secure lid. Over high heat, develop steam to high pressure. Reduce heat to maintain pressure and cook 5 minutes. Release pressure according to manufacturer's directions. Remove lid.

Add kielbasa, bell pepper, and parsley to pea soup. Bring to a boil over high heat and cook, uncovered, 3 minutes, stirring occasionally. Discard bay leaf. Makes 6 to 8 servings.

Cook's Notes: Prepared soup may be frozen up to 3 months. Thaw in refrigerator.

To quickly presoak peas, combine peas and 4 cups water in a pressure cooker. Secure lid. Over high heat, develop steam to high pressure. Turn off heat and allow steam to slowly decrease. Remove lid. Drain peas and use in soup recipe.

Rich & Creamy Borscht

Try this both chilled and warm and decide which is your favorite.

1/4 cup olive oil
4 leeks (white part only), sliced
2 carrots, diced
1/3 cup chopped parsley plus extra for
  garnish
2 large potatoes, peeled and quartered
6 large beets, peeled and quartered, greens
  trimmed
1 teaspoon salt

1/4 teaspoon white pepper
1 bay leaf
2 teaspoons dried basil, crushed between
  palms
1/2 teaspoon ground fennel
2 tablespoons prepared horseradish
5 cups chicken broth
2 tablespoons sherry
1/3 cup sour cream plus extra to serve

In a pressure cooker, heat oil. Add leeks, carrots, and parsley and sauté in hot oil 3 minutes. Add potatoes, beets, salt, pepper, bay leaf, basil, fennel, horseradish, broth, and sherry. Stir well. Secure lid. Over high heat, develop steam to high pressure. Reduce heat to maintain pressure and cook 12 minutes. Release heat according to manufacturer's directions. Remove lid. Stir beet mixture. Discard bay leaf.

Pour beet mixture into a food processor or blender. Process until smooth. Blend in sour cream.

Refrigerate until chilled or serve warm, topping individual servings with a dollop of sour cream and chopped parsley. Makes 6 servings.

Variation

Drained yogurt or low-fat sour cream may be substituted for regular sour cream.

Seasoned Croutons

Keep on hand to serve with your favorite soup.

1 cup butter, melted, or olive oil
1/2 cup grated Parmesan cheese
1/2 teaspoon dried tarragon
1/2 teaspoon dried basil

1/2 teaspoon dried oregano
1/4 teaspoon dried thyme
1 loaf French or other good-quality bread, thinly sliced

Preheat oven to 350°F (175°C).
  Combine butter, cheese, and herbs in a small bowl. Using a pastry brush, cover both sides of each bread slice with seasoned butter and place slices on a baking sheet.
  Bake 8 minutes, turn, and bake 8 minutes or until golden brown. Cut slices into small cubes.
  Set aside to cool and dry. Store in covered container. Makes 6 cups.

Cabbage Soup with Kielbasa

Green cabbage may be used in the recipe; however, the red-purple cabbage adds a delicious color to the finished soup.

1/4 cup olive oil
1 large onion, sliced
3 garlic cloves, crushed
1/4 cup chopped parsley
1 tablespoon fresh dill, minced
3 cups chicken broth
1 small head red cabbage, cored and sliced (4 cups)
1 bay leaf
3 medium-size potatoes, peeled and coarsely diced

1 tablespoon tomato paste
6 ounces smoked kielbasa, cut into bite-size pieces
1 1/4 teaspoons salt
1/4 teaspoon white pepper
1 tablespoon sugar
1/2 cup low-fat sour cream plus extra for garnish
Chopped parsley for garnish

In a pressure cooker, heat oil. Add onion, garlic, parsley, and dill and sauté in hot oil 2 minutes. Add broth, cabbage, bay leaf, potatoes, tomato paste, kielbasa, salt, pepper, and sugar. Stir well. Secure lid. Over high heat, develop steam to medium-high pressure. Reduce heat to maintain pressure and cook 4 minutes. Release pressure according to manufacturer's directions. Remove lid.

Stir vegetable mixture. Discard bay leaf. Gradually stir in sour cream. Serve hot, garnish individual servings with dollops of sour cream, and sprinkle with chopped parsley. Makes 6 servings.

Cream of Carrot Soup

Sweet and creamy, what a treat!

1/4 cup low-fat sour cream
1 teaspoon potato starch or flour
1/4 cup olive oil
1 small onion, chopped
1 garlic clove, crushed
3 cups chicken broth
8 carrots, cut into 2-inch pieces

1 1/2 tablespoons chopped fresh dill
1 tablespoon fresh lemon juice
3/4 teaspoon salt
1/4 teaspoon white pepper
1 bay leaf
Dill sprigs for garnish

Combine sour cream and potato starch in a small bowl. Set aside.

In a pressure cooker, heat oil. Add onion and garlic and sauté in hot oil 3 minutes. Add broth, carrots, dill, lemon juice, salt, pepper, and bay leaf. Secure lid. Over high heat, develop steam to high pressure. Reduce heat to maintain pressure and cook 8 minutes. Release pressure according to manufacturer's directions. Remove lid. Discard bay leaf. Pour soup into a food processor or blender. Process until smooth.

Pour puree into pressure cooker. Gradually stir in sour cream paste and simmer 1 minute, stirring. Serve hot, garnishing individual servings with dill sprigs. Makes 6 servings.

Variation

For a soup with some texture, process soup in the food processor using the pulse button a few times.

Chili

A taste of the West made easy with your pressure cooker. If only the chuckwagon cook had such conveniences on the trail!

1/2 pound dried red kidney beans
1/4 cup olive oil
1/2 pound bacon, cut into 1/2-inch pieces
2 large onions, chopped
4 garlic cloves, crushed
2 pounds coarsely ground beef
1/2 pound ground pork sausage
4 cups beef broth
1 (28-oz.) can crushed tomatoes, undrained
1/2 cup chopped green bell pepper
2 tablespoons brown sugar

2 1/2 teaspoons salt
1 teaspoon black pepper
1/2 teaspoon paprika
2 tablespoons chili powder
2 teaspoons crushed red pepper flakes
2 teaspoons ground cumin
2 tablespoons Worcestershire sauce
1/2 teaspoon hot pepper sauce (optional)
1 (8-oz.) carton low-fat sour cream
4 green onions, chopped

Place beans in a bowl and cover with enough water to measure 2 inches above beans. Soak 6 hours. Drain and set aside.

In a pressure cooker, heat oil. Add bacon, onions, and garlic and sauté in hot oil 3 minutes. Stir in beef and sausage and cook 3 minutes, stirring to break up meat. Add beans, broth, tomatoes, bell pepper, brown sugar, salt, black pepper, paprika, chili powder, pepper flakes, cumin, Worcestershire sauce, and hot pepper sauce, if using. Stir well. Secure lid. Over high heat, develop steam to high pressure, and slide a heat defuser under the pressure cooker. Reduce heat to maintain pressure and cook 13 minutes, shaking pan every 4 minutes to prevent chili from sticking.

Release pressure according to manufacturer's directions. Remove lid. Stir chili, taste, and correct seasoning as needed.

Serve hot, garnishing individual servings with a dollop of sour cream and chopped green onions. Makes 6 to 8 servings.

Variations

Use turkey bacon, ground turkey, and turkey sausage instead of regular bacon, ground beef, and pork sausage if you want a chili without beef or pork.

If you prefer a hotter flavored chili, add 2 tablespoons jalapeño salsa or 1/2 teaspoon hot pepper sauce.

Cream of Spinach & Cheddar Cheese Soup

*This appetizing first-course soup will become a favorite. Kale may be substituted
for the spinach for a different flavor.*

1 (10-oz.) package fresh spinach, cut into
   large pieces and stems removed
1/4 cup olive oil
1 medium-size onion, diced
5 cups chicken broth
1 teaspoon salt
1/2 teaspoon freshly ground white pepper
1 teaspoon dried thyme

1/4 teaspoon ground nutmeg
1 bay leaf
4 cups (16 ounces) shredded sharp Cheddar
   cheese
1/4 cup butter, softened
2 tablespoons all-purpose flour
1 (8-oz.) carton low-fat sour cream

Rinse spinach in warm water twice. Set aside to drain.

In a pressure cooker, heat oil, add onions, and sauté in hot oil over medium-high heat 2 minutes. Add broth, salt, pepper, thyme, nutmeg, bay leaf, and cheese. Layer spinach over cheese-liquid mixture. Secure lid. Over high heat, develop steam to medium-high pressure. Reduce heat to maintain pressure and cook 4 minutes. Release pressure according to manufacturer's directions. Remove lid. Stir spinach mixture well. Discard bay leaf.

Combine butter and flour, blending to paste consistency. Add, 1 tablespoon at a time, to spinach mixture and mix until thoroughly blended. Stir in sour cream. Serve hot. Makes 6 servings.

Cook's Note: Rinsing spinach in warm water wilts the leaves and releases the sand particles lodged in the leaves.

Chicken Noodle Soup

A variety of noodles are available on the market. The vermicelli noodle works deliciously in this soup.

1/4 cup olive oil
1 small onion, minced
2 cups noodles, broken into pieces
5 cups chicken broth
1 chicken breast, skin removed
2 tablespoons fresh lemon juice
1 cup chopped celery

1/4 cup chopped parsley
1 teaspoon coarse salt
1/4 teaspoon white pepper
1 bay leaf
1 teaspoon dried tarragon
Chopped parsley for garnish

In a pressure cooker, heat oil. Add onion and sauté in hot oil 2 minutes. Add noodles and cook, stirring often, 1 minute. Add broth, chicken, lemon juice, celery, parsley, salt, pepper, bay leaf, and tarragon. Secure lid. Over high heat, develop steam to high pressure. Reduce heat to maintain pressure and cook 10 minutes. Release pressure according to manufacturer's directions. Remove lid.

Remove chicken from soup. Remove chicken from bones, cut into 1-inch cubes, and add to soup, discarding bones.

Serve hot, garnishing individual servings with chopped parsley. Makes 6 servings.

Cream of Mushroom Soup

Porcini, chanterelles, morel, oyster, shiitake, and button mushrooms are all available in the supermarket at various times. Experiment with the varieties and enjoy the different flavors.

1 1/2 pounds mushrooms
1/4 cup olive oil
4 leeks (white part only), minced
1/4 cup minced parsley
2 garlic cloves, crushed
4 cups chicken broth
2 tablespoons light sherry

1 teaspoon salt
1/4 teaspoon freshly ground white pepper
1 bay leaf
1 teaspoon dried tarragon
1/4 cup butter, softened
1/4 cup all-purpose flour
1/2 cup sour cream

Clean mushrooms, removing all dirt. Cut stems from 1 pound, set stems aside, and slice caps vertically. Finely chop reserved stems with remaining 1/2 pound mushrooms.

In a pressure cooker, heat oil. Add leeks, parsley, garlic, and the finely chopped mushrooms and sauté in hot oil over high heat 3 minutes, stirring frequently. Add sliced mushrooms, broth, sherry, salt, pepper, bay leaf, and tarragon. Secure lid. Over high heat, develop steam to medium pressure. Reduce heat to maintain pressure and cook 3 minutes. Release pressure according to manufacturer's directions. Remove lid.

Combine butter and flour, mixing to paste consistency. Gradually stir sour cream into mushroom mixture. Add butter paste, 1 teaspoon at a time, stirring until paste is fully blended and soup is thickened and creamy. Serve hot. Makes 6 servings.

Potato Leek Soup

Adding the flour to the vegetables while they are sautéing enhances the rich flavor of the soup.

2 tablespoons olive oil
1/4 cup unsalted butter
4 leeks (white part only), thinly sliced
2 garlic cloves, crushed
1 large carrot, diced
4 large potatoes, thinly diced
1/4 cup minced parsley

3 tablespoons all-purpose flour
4 cups canned or fresh chicken broth
2 tablespoons bouquet garni in cheesecloth
   pouch (see page 191)
1 teaspoon coarse sea salt or granulated salt
1/4 teaspoon freshly ground white pepper
1/3 cup sour cream (optional)

In a pressure cooker, heat oil and butter. Add leeks and garlic and sauté 2 minutes. Add carrot, potatoes, and parsley; sprinkle vegetables with flour. Sauté, stirring occasionally, 2 minutes. Stir in broth and add bouquet garni, salt, and pepper. Secure lid. Over high heat, develop steam to high pressure. Reduce heat to maintain pressure and cook 8 minutes. Release pressure according to manufacturer's directions. Remove lid.

Stir in sour cream, a little at a time, if using. Bring almost to a boil, then simmer soup 5 minutes, stirring occasionally. Serve hot. Makes 6 servings.

Herbed Lamb Soup

This aromatic, flavorful soup is traditionally served to break the forty-day Easter fast.
Spring lamb is a favored tradition for the Greek Easter celebration.

1/3 cup olive oil
1 large onion, chopped
4 garlic cloves, crushed
4 lamb shanks, split in halves
5 cups chicken broth
1/2 pound lamb liver, cut into 1-inch pieces
3/4 cup rice
8 green onions, chopped
1 cup chopped celery

1 cup parsley, chopped
3/4 cup fresh dill, chopped
1 1/2 teaspoons salt
1/2 teaspoon freshly ground pepper
2 bay leaves
4 eggs
1/2 cup fresh lemon juice
1 tablespoon cornstarch

In a pressure cooker, heat oil. Add onion and garlic and sauté in hot oil over medium-high heat 3 minutes. Add lamb shanks and cook over high heat, stirring occasionally, 3 minutes. Stir in broth. Secure lid. Over high heat, develop steam to high pressure. Reduce heat to maintain pressure and cook 25 minutes. Release pressure according to manufacturer's directions. Remove lid.

Using slotted spoon, transfer lamb shanks to a platter and set aside. Combine lamb liver, rice, green onions, celery, parsley, dill, salt, pepper, and bay leaves with stock in pressure cooker. Secure lid. Over high heat, develop steam to high pressure. Reduce heat to maintain pressure and cook 8 minutes.

While vegetables cook, beat eggs about 5 minutes or until thick and creamy. Gradually blend lemon juice and cornstarch, add to eggs, and beat 1 minute.

Remove meat from lamb shank and chop into small pieces.

Release pressure according to manufacturer's directions. Remove lid. Discard bay leaves. Add lamb pieces to broth mixture. Gradually stir 1/3 cup broth from pressure cooker into egg mixture, then stir egg mixture into soup and simmer until thickened and creamy, about 1 minute. Serve hot. Makes 6 to 8 servings.

Italian Potato, Rice, & Spinach Soup

Full-bodied, almost like a stew, this Italian soup is robust and a meal by itself.

1/4 cup olive oil
6 leeks (white part only), sliced
3 garlic cloves, crushed
2 carrots, coarsely diced
1/2 cup arborio rice
3 potatoes, cut into large bite-size cubes
5 cups chicken stock
1/2 cup parsley, chopped
1/2 cup chopped celery
1 bay leaf

1 teaspoon salt
1/4 teaspoon pepper
2 teaspoons dried basil
2 tablespoons fresh lemon juice
3 tablespoons tomato paste
1 tablespoon light brown sugar
1 (10-oz.) package fresh spinach, rinsed, cut into large pieces
1/4 cup grated Parmesan cheese
1/4 cup grated Fontinella cheese

In a pressure cooker, heat oil. Add leeks, garlic, and carrots and sauté in hot oil 2 minutes. Add rice and potatoes. Stir well and cook 1 minute. Add broth, parsley, celery, bay leaf, salt, pepper, basil, lemon juice, tomato paste, and brown sugar. Stir well. Secure lid. Over high heat, develop steam to high pressure. Reduce heat to maintain pressure and cook 8 minutes. Release pressure according to manufacturer's directions. Remove lid.

   Stir soup. Lay spinach over soup. Secure lid. Over high heat, develop steam to high pressure. Reduce heat to maintain pressure, slide a heat defuser over burner, and cook 4 minutes. Release pressure according to manufacturer's directions. Remove lid.

   Stir soup well. Ladle into bowls. Combine cheeses and sprinkle over soup. Serve with hunks of Italian bread. Makes 6 to 8 servings.

Cook's Note: Freeze soup in individual containers up to 3 months. Thaw in refrigerator or microwave oven.

Manhattan Clam Chowder

*This is a family favorite. Sometimes I introduce a new flavor to this soup by adding
1/2 cup canned smoked oysters, cut into small pieces.*

1/4 cup all-purpose flour
1/4 cup butter, softened
1/4 cup olive oil
1 slice bacon, cut into 1/2-inch pieces
1 large onion, diced
3 garlic cloves, crushed
2 carrots, diced
1/2 cup diced celery
1/4 cup chopped parsley
1 cup crushed tomatoes
3 tablespoons tomato paste
4 medium-size potatoes, diced

1/4 cup chopped green bell pepper
2 tablespoons brown sugar
1 teaspoon salt
1 1/2 teaspoons dried thyme
1/2 teaspoon dried tarragon
2 bay leaves
1/2 teaspoon crushed red pepper flakes
2 dashes hot pepper sauce
1/4 cup milk
2 (10-oz.) cans minced clams, liquid strained
  into fish stock
2 cups Rich Fish Stock (page 23)

Make a paste by blending flour into butter; set aside.

In a pressure cooker, heat oil. Add bacon, onion, garlic, carrots, celery, and parsley and sauté in hot oil 3 minutes. Add tomatoes, tomato paste, potatoes, bell pepper, brown sugar, salt, thyme, tarragon, bay leaves, pepper flakes, hot pepper sauce, milk, and fish stock mixture. Stir well. Secure lid. Over high heat, develop steam to high pressure. Reduce heat to maintain pressure and cook 5 minutes. Release pressure according to manufacturer's directions. Remove lid.

Stir clams into vegetable mixture and cook over medium-high heat 3 minutes. Discard bay leaves.

Stir paste into soup and cook 1 minute, stirring, or until soup is thickened and creamy. Serve hot. Makes 6 to 8 servings.

New England Clam Chowder

Creamy and rich, this is the traditional clam chowder enhanced with herbs and sour cream.

1/4 cup olive oil
3 leeks (white part only), sliced
2 garlic cloves, crushed
2 carrots, coarsely diced
1/2 cup coarsely diced celery
1/4 cup chopped parsley
2 (10-oz.) cans minced clams, strained, with
   liquid added to fish stock
2 1/2 cups Rich Fish Stock (page 23)
4 potatoes, peeled and diced

1 teaspoon salt
1/4 teaspoon freshly ground white pepper
2 tablespoons bouquet garni in cheesecloth
   bag (see page 191)
2 bay leaves
1/4 cup all-purpose flour
1 cup half-and-half or milk
1/4 cup sour cream
1/4 cup butter, softened

In a pressure cooker, heat oil. Add leeks, garlic, carrots, celery, and parsley and sauté in hot oil 3 minutes. Add stock with clam liquid, potatoes, salt, pepper, bouquet garni, and bay leaves. Stir thoroughly. Secure lid. Over high heat, develop steam to high pressure. Reduce heat to maintain pressure and cook 5 minutes. Release pressure according to manufacturer's directions. Remove lid. Discard bouquet garni bag.

   Stir in clams. Cook over medium-high heat 2 minutes, stirring frequently. Remove from heat and discard bay leaves.

   Combine flour, half-and-half, sour cream, and butter, whisking to combine. Gradually add paste to clam mixture and cook 1 minute, stirring, or until thickened and creamy. Serve hot. Makes 6 servings.

Variation

To reduce fat, skim milk and low-fat sour cream may be added at the end, substituting for half-and-half and regular sour cream. Simply make a paste with flour and blend into soup.

Onion Soup with Gnocchi Parmesan Dumplings

An Italian classic made easier.

Dumplings (see opposite)
1/3 cup olive oil
8 medium-size onions, sliced
2 teaspoons minced garlic
4 cups chicken broth
1 teaspoon coarse salt
1/2 teaspoon freshly ground white pepper
1 bay leaf
3/4 teaspoon dried thyme
2 tablespoons gin (optional)
1/2 cup grated Parmesan cheese
Chopped Italian parsley to garnish

Dumplings:
1/2 cup water
2 cups potatoes, peeled, cut into 2-inch pieces
1 tablespoon sour cream
1 green onion, minced
1/4 cup grated Parmesan cheese
3 tablespoons butter
1/3 cup unbleached all-purpose flour
2 egg whites
1/2 teaspoon salt
1/8 teaspoon freshly ground pepper

Prepare dumpling mixture.

In a pressure cooker, heat oil. Add onions and sauté in hot oil 3 minutes. Add garlic, broth, salt, pepper, bay leaf, and thyme. Secure lid. Over high heat, develop steam to medium pressure. Reduce heat to maintain pressure and cook 2 minutes. Release pressure according to manufacturer's directions. Remove lid.

Discard bay leaf. Bring soup to a rolling boil over high heat and cook 2 minutes. Reduce heat to medium-high, add gin, if using, and stir. Reduce heat to medium.

Drop small teaspoonfuls of dumpling mixture into soup. Cook 2 minutes. Serve hot, sprinkling individual servings with cheese and garnishing with parsley. Makes 6 to 8 servings.

Dumplings

Pour water into pressure cooker. Place potatoes in steam basket and insert in pressure cooker. Secure lid. Over high heat, develop steam to high pressure. Reduce range heat to medium and cook 6 minutes. Release pressure according to manufacturer's directions. Remove lid.

Drain potatoes and place in a bowl. Add sour cream, green onion, and cheese. Using an electric mixer, whip until creamy. Add butter and flour and blend well. Wash mixer beaters. Whip egg whites until soft peaks form. Fold into potato mixture. Season with salt and pepper. Set potato mixture aside.

Cook's Note: Gnocchi may be piped out of a 16-inch pastry bag fitted with a 1/2-inch pastry tube. Squeeze bag and cut off 2-inch pieces into soup.

Lentil Soup

The white wine vinegar adds a zesty flavor. It is often added to Mediterranean legume dishes.

1 pound lentils
1/4 cup olive oil
2 medium-size onions, minced
3 garlic cloves, crushed
6 cups chicken broth or water
2 carrots, finely diced
1 cup coarsely chopped celery

1/4 cup tomato paste
1 tablespoon brown sugar
1 1/2 teaspoons salt
3/4 teaspoon white pepper
2 bay leaves
1 teaspoon dried tarragon
2 tablespoons white wine vinegar

Place lentils in a bowl. Add enough water to measure 2 inches above lentils. Soak 4 hours. Drain.
 In a pressure cooker, heat oil. Add onions and garlic and sauté in hot oil 3 to 4 minutes. Stir in drained lentils. Add broth, carrots, celery, tomato paste, brown sugar, salt, pepper, bay leaves, and tarragon. Stir well. Secure lid. Over high heat, develop steam to high pressure. Reduce heat to maintain pressure and cook 12 minutes. Release pressure according to manufacturer's directions. Remove lid.
 Cook over high heat 1 minute. Stir in vinegar. Discard bay leaves. Serve hot. Makes 6 servings.

South-of-the-Border Black Bean Soup

This hearty black bean soup makes it easy to follow the new dietary guidelines,
which tell us to eat more beans, pasta, and rice.

3/4 pound dried black beans
1/4 cup olive oil
1/2 pound smoked bacon, cut into 1/2-inch
  pieces
1 large onion, diced
2 garlic cloves, crushed
1/3 cup chopped cilantro
1 1/2 teaspoons coarse sea salt or granulated
  salt
2 bay leaves
2 teaspoons chili powder

1 teaspoon dried oregano
1 teaspoon crushed red pepper flakes
1/2 teaspoon ground cumin
5 cups beef broth
2 tablespoons tomato paste
2 tablespoons brown sugar
2 teaspoons Worcestershire sauce
1/8 teaspoon hot pepper sauce
1 cup (4 ounces) shredded Monterey Jack
  cheese

Place beans into a bowl. Add enough water to measure 2 inches above beans. Soak 4 hours. Drain beans.

In a pressure cooker, heat oil. Add bacon and cook until crisp. Add onion and garlic and sauté 3 minutes. Add beans, cilantro, salt, bay leaves, chili powder, oregano, pepper flakes, cumin, broth, tomato paste, brown sugar, Worcestershire sauce, and hot pepper sauce. Stir until thoroughly mixed. Secure lid. Over high heat, develop steam to high pressure. Reduce heat to maintain pressure and cook 18 minutes.

Release pressure according to manufacturer's directions. Remove lid. Stir soup. Discard bay leaves. Either serve soup chunky or pour soup into a food processor or blender and process to puree.

Serve hot, garnishing individual servings with cheese. Makes 6 to 8 servings.

Variations

To reduce the fat, substitute turkey bacon for regular bacon.
Cheese garnish may be omitted.

Cook's Note: Prepared soup may be frozen up to 3 months. Thaw in refrigerator.

Spicy Chicken Corn Chowder

This Southwest chowder is a favorite and full of great flavors.

1/4 pound bacon, cut into 1-inch pieces
1/4 cup olive oil
1 large onion, diced
3 garlic cloves, slivered
2 chicken breasts
1 (16-oz.) can crushed tomatoes
1/4 cup jalapeño salsa
1 green bell pepper, coarsely chopped
2 cups chicken broth
1 teaspoon salt

1/2 teaspoon crushed red pepper flakes
1/8 teaspoon hot pepper sauce
2 (8- to 10-oz.) packages frozen whole-kernel corn
1/2 cup chopped cilantro
1 tablespoon sherry
3 tablespoons all-purpose flour
3 tablespoons butter, softened
1 cup half-and-half

In a pressure cooker, sauté bacon until crisp. Add oil, onion, garlic, and chicken. Sauté 3 minutes. Stir in tomatoes, salsa, bell pepper, broth, salt, pepper flakes, and hot pepper sauce.

Secure lid. Over high heat, develop steam to high pressure. Reduce heat to maintain pressure and cook 6 minutes. Release pressure according to manufacturer's directions. Remove lid. Lift chicken out. Remove meat from bone and cut into bite-size pieces.

Add chicken, corn, cilantro, and sherry to the soup. Bring to a simmer and cook 2 minutes. Combine flour and butter, blending to paste consistency. Add 1 tablespoon at a time, mixing until soup appears creamy, and cook 1 more minute. Gradually stir in half-and-half and mix thoroughly. Serve hot with corn chips. Makes 6 to 8 servings.

Variation

Substitute drained low-fat yogurt blended with flour for the half-and-half. Omit butter.

Split Pea Soup with Ham

Split pea soup is traditionally made with a ham bone.

1 pound dried split green peas
1/4 cup olive oil
1 large onion, diced
2 teaspoons minced or crushed garlic
1 ham bone or 4 slices smoked bacon, cut into
   1/2-inch pieces
5 cups canned or fresh chicken broth
1 tablespoon lemon juice

2 tablespoons bouquet garni in cheesecloth
   pouch (see page 191)
1 bay leaf
1/2 cup diced carrot
1 medium-size potato, diced
1 teaspoon sea salt
1/2 teaspoon freshly ground white pepper
1/2 cup diced smoked ham

Place peas in bowl. Add enough water to measure 2 inches above peas. Soak 6 hours. Drain peas.

In a pressure cooker, heat oil. Add onion and garlic and sauté in hot oil 3 minutes. Add ham bone (if using bacon, cook 3 minutes), broth, lemon juice, bouquet garni, and bay leaf.

Secure lid. Over high heat, develop steam to high pressure. Reduce heat to maintain pressure and cook 15 minutes. Release pressure according to manufacturer's directions. Remove lid. Add carrot, potato, peas, salt, and pepper. Secure lid. Over high heat, develop steam to high pressure. Reduce heat to maintain pressure and cook 8 minutes. Release pressure according to manufacturer's directions. Remove lid.

Remove bouquet garni bag. Stir soup with a wooden spoon. Add ham pieces and mix well. Using slotted spoon or large tongs, remove ham bone. Serve hot. Makes 6 to 8 servings.

Variation

If on a low-fat diet, substitute turkey bacon and use vegetable stock.

Cook's Note: Soup may be frozen up to 1 month. Thaw in refrigerator.

Vegetable Soup with Sausage Bits

This family favorite is thick and hearty. To reduce calories and fat,
use turkey sausage and turkey bacon. You'll love the flavors.

1/3 cup olive oil
1/2 pound bacon, cut into 1-inch pieces
2 large onions, sliced
3 garlic cloves, crushed
2 carrots, cut into bite-size pieces
1 tablespoon all-purpose flour
1/2 pound breakfast sausage links, cut into
   1-inch pieces
4 celery stalks, cut into 1-inch pieces
4 medium-size potatoes, peeled and cut into
   1-inch cubes
6 cups beef broth
1/4 pound uncooked vermicelli pasta, broken
   into small pieces

3 tablespoons tomato paste
2 tablespoons lemon juice
1 tablespoon light brown sugar
2 teaspoons coarse salt
1/2 teaspoon freshly ground pepper
2 teaspoons dried oregano
1 teaspoon dried basil
1 bay leaf
1/2 cup chopped parsley
1 cup frozen green peas
1 cup cooked garbanzo beans (chickpeas)
   (page 138)

In a pressure cooker, heat oil. Add bacon, onions, and garlic and sauté in hot oil 4 minutes. Add carrots, sprinkle with flour, and cook, stirring, 2 minutes. Add sausage, celery, potatoes, broth, vermicelli, tomato paste, lemon juice, brown sugar, salt, pepper, oregano, basil, and bay leaf. Stir until thoroughly mixed. Secure lid. Over high heat, develop steam to high pressure. Reduce heat to maintain pressure and cook 8 minutes. Release pressure according to manufacturer's directions. Remove lid.

  Add parsley, peas, and beans to vegetable mixture. Cook over medium-high heat 4 minutes, stirring occasionally. Serve hot with Seasoned Croutons (page 26). Makes 6 to 8 servings.

Salads

The pressure cooker will indeed hasten recipe completion.

This chapter includes an assortment of ideas developed into tested recipes combining fresh vegetables, fruit, and pressure-cooked poultry along with pasta, rice, and legumes. The salads are light and garnished with flavor-filled dressings that tantalize the palate of the most discriminating diner.

Using vegetables in their proper season will allow you to enjoy the ultimate in flavor and nutrient value, not to mention the lower cost.

Experiment with the new exotic greens such as red radicchio from Italy, lemon-tart arugula, or tender mâche, pressure cooked in combination with poached chicken or rice.

The recipes within this section will be the beginning of an adventure in using pressure cooking to prepare your favorite fruits and vegetables, leading to new and delicious salads.

Calabria Green Bean Salad

This recipe was developed from one my daughter-in-law brought from her home in Calabria, Italy.

1/4 cup olive oil
2 green onions, sliced
1 cup water
1 tablespoon sugar
3/4 teaspoon salt
1/8 teaspoon pepper
1/2 teaspoon dried basil
1 pound green beans, ends removed
8 cherry tomatoes, cut into halves

4 garlic cloves, thinly sliced
Dressing (see below)

Dressing:
1/4 cup extra-virgin olive oil
2 tablespoons lemon juice
1 tablespoon white vinegar
1/4 teaspoon salt

In a pressure cooker, heat oil. Add green onions and sauté in hot oil 1 minute. Add water, sugar, salt, pepper, and basil. Stir in beans. Secure lid. Over high heat, develop steam to medium-high pressure. Reduce heat to maintain pressure and cook 1 minute. Quickly release pressure according to manufacturer's directions. Remove lid.

Drain beans in a colander, rinsing under cold, running water. Place in a bowl and add tomatoes and garlic. Prepare dressing. Drizzle over vegetables and toss gently to coat. Makes 6 servings.

Dressing
Whisk oil, lemon juice, vinegar, and salt together until slightly thickened.

Cook's Notes: Recipe may be increased or decreased.
Select beans that are crisp, firm, and free of blemishes.

Carrot Garbanzo Bean Salad

The garlic-laced dressing accents a cooked carrot and garbanzo bean salad.
You'll find lots of uses for this dressing.

1 cup water
6 carrots, cut into julienne strips
Dash of salt
1 cup cooked garbanzo beans (chickpeas)
 (page 138)
3 green onions, minced
Greek Salad Dressing (see below)

Greek Salad Dressing:

1 1/2 cups extra-virgin olive oil
1/2 cup vegetable oil

1/2 cup white wine vinegar
1/4 cup fresh lemon juice
1/4 cup mayonnaise
5 garlic cloves, crushed
1 teaspoon salt
1/2 teaspoon freshly ground pepper
1 tablespoon dried oregano
1 teaspoon dried rosemary
1 teaspoon prepared mustard

Pour water into a pressure cooker. Layer carrots in steam basket and insert basket into cooker. Sprinkle with salt. Secure lid. Over high heat, develop steam to medium pressure. Reduce heat to maintain pressure and cook 2 minutes. Release pressure according to manufacturer's directions. Remove lid.

 Drain carrots in a colander, rinsing under cold, running water. Drain well. Combine carrots, garbanzo beans, and green onions in serving bowl. Prepare dressing. Pour 1/4 cup dressing over vegetables and toss to coat. Refrigerate remaining dressing for another use. Makes 6 servings.

Greek Salad Dressing

Combine oils, vinegar, lemon juice, mayonnaise, garlic, salt, pepper, oregano, rosemary, and mustard in a food processor or blender. Process until smooth.

 Pour dressing into a jar with tight-fitting lid. Store leftovers in refrigerator. Shake well before using. Makes about 3 cups.

Cook's Note: Scrub carrots under cool running water using a vegetable brush. Unless the skin is thick there is no need to peel carrots.

German Potato Salad with Sausage

The smoky taste from the bacon, whether pork or turkey, is an important factor in the flavor of the salad.

3 slices regular or turkey bacon, cut into 1-inch pieces
1 medium-size onion, cut into 1/8-inch slices
2 garlic cloves, crushed
1/3 cup chicken broth
1/3 cup white wine vinegar
3/4 teaspoon salt
1/4 teaspoon white pepper
1/4 teaspoon dried dill weed

5 medium-size potatoes, peeled and cut into 1/2-inch slices
1 pound cooked bratwurst or turkey sausage, cut into 1-inch pieces
1/2 cup regular or light sour cream
1/2 teaspoon dry mustard
1 green bell pepper, diced
4 radishes, thinly sliced
1/3 cup minced parsley

In a pressure cooker, sauté bacon 2 minutes or until crisp. Stir in onion and garlic and cook 2 minutes. Add broth, vinegar, salt, white pepper, and dill; mix thoroughly. Add potatoes and sausage and stir well. Secure lid. Over high heat, develop steam to medium-high pressure. Reduce heat to maintain pressure and cook 4 minutes. Release pressure according to manufacturer's directions. Remove lid.

Stir potato-sausage mixture carefully but thoroughly. Add sour cream, mustard, bell pepper, radishes, and parsley, tossing gently to mix.

Pour salad into a serving bowl and serve warm or chilled. Makes 6 to 8 servings.

Beets in Dilled Horseradish Sauce

Horseradish sauce makes a tangy dressing for this beet salad.

1 tablespoon prepared horseradish sauce
2 tablespoons sour cream
1/4 cup extra-virgin olive oil
1/2 teaspoon salt
Dash of white pepper

1 teaspoon dill weed or 2 tablespoons chopped fresh dill
4 large beets, pressure cooked (page 132) and chilled
Fresh dill sprigs for garnish (optional)

Combine horseradish sauce, sour cream, oil, salt, pepper, and dill in a measuring cup with a spout. Whisk until well blended.

  Cut beets into bite-size wedges and place in a salad bowl. Pour sauce over beets, tossing gently to coat. Garnish with dill sprigs. Makes 6 servings.

Cook's Note: Store uncooked beets in a paper bag in the refrigerator to control moisture and prevent rotting.

Mediterranean Beet Salad

Pressure-cooked beets are more flavorful than boiled beets and the color is incredibly deep and beautiful.

4 beets, pressure cooked (page 132)
1 onion, cut crosswise into thin slices and
  separated into rings
1/2 cup pitted ripe olives
1 small cucumber, peeled, seeds removed, and
  cut into 1-inch slices
Mint Dressing (see opposite)
1/4 pound goat cheese or feta cheese, sliced

Mint Dressing:
1/4 cup extra-virgin olive oil
1 tablespoon fresh lemon juice
1/4 teaspoon salt
1 tablespoon dried spearmint, crushed between
  palms
1 teaspoon dried oregano, crushed between
  palms

Peel and slice beets. Combine with onion, olives, and cucumber in a salad bowl. Prepare dressing and pour over vegetables, gently tossing until thoroughly mixed.

  Garnish salad with cheese slices. Makes 6 servings.

Mint Dressing
Combine oil, lemon juice, and seasonings in measuring cup with spout. Whisk until thoroughly blended.

Variation

Substitute thin shaving of Parmesan or Fontinella cheese for the goat cheese.

Middle Eastern Beet Salad

Beautiful and delicious, the spearmint dressing adds a cooling touch.

Dressing (see opposite)
6 large beets, pressure cooked (page 132)
1 green bell pepper, thinly sliced lengthwise
1 small onion, cut crosswise into thin slices and separated into rings
1/2 cup coarsely chopped parsley
1 small cucumber, peeled, seeds removed, and cut into bite-size pieces
2 ripe tomatoes, halved, seeds removed, and diced
2 pita bread rounds, toasted and cut into bite-size squares (see Cook's Note, below)

Dressing:
1/3 cup extra-virgin olive oil
2 tablespoons fresh lemon juice
1/2 teaspoon salt
1/8 teaspoon white pepper
2 garlic cloves, crushed
1 teaspoon dried spearmint, crushed between palms

Prepare dressing and set aside.
   Peel beets and cut each into 8 wedges. Combine with bell pepper, onion, parsley, cucumber, tomatoes, and bread pieces in a salad bowl; toss gently to combine
   Drizzle dressing over salad and toss gently to coat with dressing. Makes 6 servings.

Dressing
Combine oil, lemon juice, salt, pepper, garlic, and spearmint in a measuring cup with a spout. Whisk until thoroughly blended.

Cook's Note: Pita bread is a flat Arabic bread and is very low in fat. Place bread on a baking sheet, brush with a little olive oil, and bake in a 375°F (190°C) oven 8 minutes. Cut into squares.

Apricot & Chicken Salad with Orange Dressing

The dressing is the cinnamon and orange flavored cooking juices.

3 whole chicken breasts, skin removed
1 cup orange juice
1/4 cup sugar
1 cinnamon stick
16 dried apricots, quartered

Arugula, Boston, or red-leaf lettuce leaves
6 slices Swiss cheese, cut into 3-inch strips
1 (11-oz.) can mandarin oranges, drained well
1/2 cup slivered almonds, toasted (see Cook's Note, page 158)

In a pressure cooker, combine chicken breasts, orange juice, sugar, cinnamon stick, and apricots. Secure lid. Over high heat, develop steam to high pressure. Reduce heat to maintain pressure and cook 10 minutes. Release pressure according to manufacturer's directions. Remove lid.

Place chicken pieces on a cutting board. Using a slotted spoon, transfer apricots to a bowl. Remove chicken from bone, cut into bite-size pieces, and discard bones.

Place lettuce leaves on each individual plate. Arrange chicken pieces on lettuce, add a few strips of cheese, and top with apricots, mandarin oranges, and almonds. Drizzle cooking juices over top of salad. Makes 6 servings.

Chinese Chicken Salad with Sesame Dressing

Be adventurous and try cooked basmati or arborio rice for the salad.

2 cups Pressure Steamed Rice (page 146)
2 cups cubed cooked chicken (page 91)
1 (6-oz.) can water chestnuts, drained well and thinly sliced
1 pound snow peas, ends and any strings removed
2 celery stalks, diced
2 green onions, diced
Sesame Dressing (see opposite)

Sesame Dressing:

1/3 cup vegetable oil
1 tablespoon sesame oil
1 teaspoon soy sauce
1 teaspoon white wine vinegar
1 garlic clove, crushed
1/2 teaspoon salt

Combine rice, chicken, and vegetables in a salad bowl, gently tossing to combine. Prepare dressing and pour over salad, tossing to thoroughly coat. Makes 4 servings.

Sesame Dressing
Combine oils, soy sauce, vinegar, garlic, and salt in a measuring cup with a spout. Whisk until well blended.

Red Kidney Bean Salad

The salad is great for picnics or barbecues.

1/2 pound dried red kidney beans
4 cups water
1 teaspoon salt
2 carrots, coarsely grated
1 small red onion, cut crosswise into thin slices
   and separated into rings
1/4 cup chopped parsley
1 teaspoon oregano
Dressing (see opposite)

Dressing:
1/3 cup extra-virgin olive oil
2 tablespoons fresh lemon juice
1 teaspoon white wine vinegar
1/2 teaspoon salt
Dash of white pepper

Place beans in a bowl. Add enough water to measure 2 inches above beans. Soak 4 hours or overnight. Drain.

In a pressure cooker, combine drained beans, 4 cups water, and salt. Secure lid. Over high heat, develop steam to high pressure. Reduce heat to maintain pressure and cook 13 minutes. Release pressure according to manufacturer's directions. Remove lid.

Drain beans in a colander, rinsing under cold, running water until beans are cool.

Combine beans, carrots, onion, and parsley in a salad bowl. Sprinkle with oregano. Prepare dressing. Drizzle over vegetables and toss to thoroughly mix. Makes 8 servings.

Dressing
Combine oil, lemon juice, vinegar, salt, and pepper in a measuring cup with a spout. Whisk until thoroughly blended.

Warm Garbanzo Bean Salad

Great for parties, garbanzo bean salad originated in Italy.
The salad is also delicious served chilled, eliminating the baking.

3 cups cooked garbanzo beans (chickpeas)
  (page 138)
3 green onions, chopped
1 small red onion, sliced in rings
1/2 cup chopped green bell pepper
1/2 cup minced parsley
1 carrot, coarsely grated
Dressing (see opposite)
1/4 cup freshly grated Parmesan or Romano
  cheese

Dressing:
1/4 cup extra-virgin olive oil
2 teaspoons fresh lemon juice
2 teaspoons white wine vinegar
1 tablespoon mayonnaise
2 garlic cloves, crushed
1/4 teaspoon salt
Dash of freshly ground white pepper
1/2 teaspoon dried oregano

Preheat oven to 375°F (190°C). Combine beans, green onions, red onion, bell pepper, parsley, and carrot in an ovenproof bowl. Toss gently to mix thoroughly.

Prepare dressing. Add dressing a little at a time, tossing gently to coat vegetables, until reaching your preferred taste. Sprinkle salad with cheese and toss gently.

Bake 6 minutes. Stir and serve. Makes 6 servings.

Dressing
Combine oil, lemon juice, vinegar, mayonnaise, garlic, salt, pepper, and oregano in a measuring cup with a spout. Whisk until thoroughly blended.

Warm Spinach Salad

This wilted spinach salad is topped with tomatoes and goat cheese.

1/4 cup olive oil
6 green onions, chopped
1 garlic clove, crushed
2 (10-oz.) packages fresh spinach, rinsed well
1 cup water
2 teaspoons salt
1 teaspoon dried rosemary
1/3 cup chopped parsley
2 large tomatoes, halved, seeds removed, and
  cubed

1/2 pound goat cheese or feta cheese, sliced
Dressing (see below)

Dressing:
1/4 cup extra-virgin olive oil
1 tablespoon fresh lemon juice
1/2 teaspoon salt
Dash of pepper

In a pressure cooker, heat oil. Add green onions and garlic and sauté in oil 2 minutes. Stir in spinach. Add water, salt, and rosemary. Secure lid. Over high heat, develop steam to high pressure. Reduce heat to maintain pressure and cook 2 minutes. Release pressure according to manufacturer's directions. Remove lid.

Drain spinach in a colander. Using a spatula, gently press spinach leaves against side of colander to extract excess water. Place spinach in a bowl and sprinkle with parsley. Add tomatoes and toss gently.

Arrange vegetables in a serving dish and top with cheese slices. Prepare dressing. Spoon dressing over cheese. Makes 6 to 8 servings.

Dressing
Combine oil, lemon juice, salt, and pepper in a small bowl. Whisk until well blended.

Warm Lamb Salad with Peppers & Feta Cheese

Made with lamb, this main dish salad is perfect for a summer luncheon.

1/4 cup olive oil
1 1/2 pounds lamb steaks (1 inch thick)
1 small onion, minced
2 garlic cloves, crushed
1 cup chicken broth or stock
1 tablespoon fresh lemon juice
1 tablespoon sugar
1 1/2 teaspoons salt
1/2 teaspoon pepper
1 teaspoon dried dill weed
1 teaspoon dried oregano
2 green bell peppers, sliced
1/3 cup chopped parsley

2 cups (8 ounces) crumbled feta cheese or
  shaved Fontinella or Parmesan cheese
Yogurt Dressing (see below)
Lettuce leaves

Yogurt Dressing:
1/4 cup extra-virgin olive oil
1/4 cup plain yogurt
1 tablespoon fresh lemon juice
1 garlic clove, crushed
1/2 teaspoon salt
1/2 teaspoon dried dill weed

In a pressure cooker, heat oil. Add steaks and sauté in hot oil, turning to brown on both sides. Transfer steaks to a platter. Add onion and garlic and sauté in hot oil 2 minutes. Add steaks, broth, lemon juice, sugar, salt, pepper, dill, and oregano. Stir well. Secure lid. Over high heat, develop steam to high pressure. Reduce heat to maintain pressure and cook 10 minutes. Release pressure according to manufacturer's directions. Remove lid.

Remove steaks and place on a cutting board. Add bell pepper to cooking liquid. Secure lid. Over high heat, develop steam to medium pressure. Reduce heat to maintain pressure at low and cook 2 minutes. Release pressure according to manufacturer's directions. Remove lid.

Drain bell peppers in a colander. Cut lamb into 2-inch slices. Combine lamb, bell pepper, parsley, and cheese in a salad bowl. Toss gently.

Prepare dressing. Arrange lettuce leaves on a serving platter and top with lamb mixture. Drizzle 2 tablespoons dressing over salad. Serve remaining dressing on the side. Makes 6 servings.

Yogurt Dressing
Combine oil, yogurt, lemon juice, garlic, salt, and dill in a jar with a tight-fitting lid. Shake until thoroughly blended. Store in refrigerator.

Beef, Pork, Lamb, & Veal

You'll forget about expensive cuts of meats, heavily marbled with fat, when you use the pressure cooker. Pressure cooking transforms the leaner, tougher cuts of meat into tender morsels that can be cut with a fork. You can be assured that nutrients are retained, along with wonderful, pronounced flavors.

As the liquid comes to a boil and the steam trapped beneath the tight lid begins to penetrate the meat, it begins to break down the muscle and protein, gradually tenderizing the meat.

Following the recommended guidelines for preparation will assure ultimate flavor and retain nutrients.

SELECTING MEAT

The U.S. Department of Agriculture (USDA) grading system of meat is based on maturity and the amount of fat.

- **U.S. Prime:** Well-marbled with fat and therefore usually very tender. Save your money, as this grade does not require pressure cooking to tenderize.
- **U.S. Choice:** Grade most available in all grocery chains. It works extremely well in the pressure cooker.
- **U.S. Good:** Less expensive than prime and choice grades, it contains more muscle and is much leaner, with lower fat content. It works very well in pressure cooked recipes but does require a longer cooking time to tenderize.
- **U.S. Select:** A new rating, this grade of meat is lean, low in fat, and tender.

BUYING MEAT

- **Beef:** Look for a red, firm surface. Fat marbling should be evenly distributed and excess fat trimmed from edges.
- **Pork:** Make sure it is USDA graded. Look for a light pink color. Fat marbling should be evenly distributed and excess fat trimmed from edges.
- **Lamb:** Look for dark pink to red moist surface, avoiding dark red meat. Lamb has less fat marbling than beef and pork; fat should be trimmed from edges.
- **Veal:** Look for delicate whitish pink surface, finely marbled with very little fat at edges.

COOKING TIPS

- Make sure meat is cut into uniform pieces to ensure even cooking.
- Brown meat to seal in the natural juices and add rich color and flavor.
- Reduce the steam slowly at the end of the cooking cycle.

TIMING CHART FOR MEAT

Beef

12 to 15 minutes per inch
- Oxtail (for stocks)
- Short ribs
- Stewing beef
- Blade roast
- Chuck roast
- Flank steak
- Corned beef
- Shanks

20 minutes per inch
- Brisket

Pork

15 minutes per inch
- Hocks
- Shoulder
- Riblets
- Chops

Lamb

10 minutes per inch
- Neck
- Shanks
- Riblets
- Shoulder

Veal

8 minutes per inch
- Breast
- Rump
- Steak
- Shoulder
- Stew

Beef Stroganoff

This lovely combination of beef thinly sliced in a rich sauce
is named after a Russian, Count Stroganoff. It is traditionally served with rice or buttered noodles.

1/4 cup olive oil
1 large onion, sliced
2 garlic cloves, crushed
1 1/2 pounds stewing beef, thinly sliced
1/2 cup beef broth
2 tablespoons sherry
1/3 cup chopped parsley
1 teaspoon salt
1/8 teaspoon freshly ground pepper

1 teaspoon dried tarragon
1 pound mushrooms, sliced
2 medium-size tomatoes, cut into eighths and
   seeds removed
1/2 cup sour cream
1/2 teaspoon prepared mustard
2 tablespoons potato starch or flour
Cooked noodles (page 130) or rice (page
   129)

In a pressure cooker, heat oil. Add onion and garlic and sauté in hot oil 3 minutes. Add beef, stir, and cook 2 minutes. Stir in broth, sherry, parsley, salt, pepper, and tarragon. Secure lid. Over high heat, develop steam to high pressure. Reduce heat to maintain pressure and cook 18 minutes. Release pressure according to manufacturer's directions. Remove lid.

Stir mushrooms and tomatoes into beef mixture. Secure lid. Over high heat, develop steam to medium pressure. Reduce heat to maintain pressure and cook 1 minute. Release pressure according to manufacturer's directions. Remove lid.

Cook beef and vegetable mixture over high heat 1 minute. Combine sour cream, mustard, and potato starch in a small bowl. Gradually add to beef and vegetable mixture and cook, stirring, until slightly thickened.

Serve with noodles. Makes 6 servings.

Brisket of Beef with Vegetables & Horseradish Sauce

The brisket comes from the breast of the animal and is sold without bone.
The flat cut has less fat than the pointed cut.

1/3 cup olive oil
1 3-lb. beef brisket (flat cut)
2 onions, sliced
4 garlic cloves, quartered
2 carrots, sliced
2 cups beef broth
2 tablespoons fresh lemon juice
2 tablespoons tomato paste
1/3 cup chopped parsley
1 teaspoon salt
1/2 teaspoon pepper

2 bay leaves
6 potatoes, peeled and quartered
3 carrots, cut into 2-inch pieces
Horseradish Sauce (see below)

Horseradish Sauce:

1/3 cup sour cream
3 tablespoons butter, softened
2 tablespoons prepared horseradish
2 tablespoons potato starch or flour

In a pressure cooker, heat oil. Add brisket and brown in hot oil on both sides, turning with long-handled tongs. Remove meat and set aside. Add onions, garlic, and sliced carrots and sauté in hot oil 3 minutes, stirring and scraping bottom of cooker to loosen any browned particles of meat. Stir in broth, lemon juice, tomato paste, parsley, salt, pepper, and bay leaves. Add meat. Secure lid. Over high heat, develop steam to high pressure. Reduce heat to maintain pressure and cook 1 hour. Release pressure according to manufacturer's directions. Remove lid.

Stir potatoes and carrot pieces into meat mixture. Secure lid. Over high heat, develop steam to high pressure. Reduce heat to maintain pressure and cook 9 minutes. Prepare sauce and set aside. Release pressure according to manufacturer's directions. Remove lid.

Using a slotted spoon, transfer meat and vegetables to a platter. Loosely cover to retain heat.

Strain cooking liquid through a fine sieve and return liquid to pressure cooker. Whisk in horseradish sauce and cook over medium heat 1 minute until thickened, stirring frequently.

Slice brisket. Serve sauce with brisket and vegetables. Makes 6 servings.

Horseradish Sauce
Combine sour cream, butter, horseradish, and potato starch in a small bowl. Blend until smooth.

Corned Beef Brisket with Vegetables & Horseradish Sauce

The point on the brisket indicates it has more fat and cooks up to be tender.
Sliced thin, it makes lovely corned beef sandwiches.

4 cups water
1 (2 1/2-lb.) corned beef brisket, uniformly shaped with point at one end
3 garlic cloves, quartered
2 bay leaves
4 carrots, cut into 3-inch pieces
1 head cabbage, cut into 6 wedges
6 potatoes, peeled and quartered
3 turnips, peeled and quartered
Horseradish Sauce (see below)

Horseradish Sauce:

1/3 cup prepared horseradish
1 teaspoon prepared mustard
1/4 cup sour cream
1 tablespoon lemon juice
2 garlic cloves, crushed
2 tablespoons minced green onions (green part only)
1 teaspoon sugar
1/2 teaspoon salt
1/8 teaspoon white pepper

Pour water into a pressure cooker. Add brisket. Over high heat, bring water to a rolling boil. Skim residue from surface. Add garlic and bay leaves. Secure lid. Over high heat, develop steam to high pressure. Reduce heat to maintain pressure and cook 1 hour and 15 minutes. Release pressure according to manufacturer's directions. Remove lid.

Add vegetables to brisket and liquid, stirring gently. Secure lid. Over high heat, develop steam to high pressure. Reduce heat to maintain pressure and cook 6 minutes. Release pressure according to manufacturer's directions. Remove lid.

Prepare Horseradish Sauce. Transfer vegetables to a platter. Slice brisket across the grain and arrange slices on a platter. Serve with Horseradish Sauce. Makes 6 servings.

Horseradish Sauce
Combine horseradish, mustard, sour cream, and lemon juice in a bowl; blend thoroughly. Add garlic, green onions, sugar, salt, and white pepper and mix well. Serve sauce with corned beef, roast beef, or roast pork.

Far East Pepper Steak

The pepper flakes in this dish with a hint of the Orient may be a little hot to the palate.
If you prefer a less spicy flavor, omit the red pepper flakes.

1 tablespoon sesame oil
2 tablespoons olive oil
1 large onion, sliced
3 garlic cloves, sliced
1 pound beef round steak, cut into 3" x 1/2"
  strips
1/2 cup beef broth or stock
1 tablespoon sherry
1 teaspoon light brown sugar
1/2 teaspoon salt

1 teaspoon grated ginger root
1/2 teaspoon red pepper flakes
2 tomatoes, cut into eighths and seeds removed
1 green bell pepper, sliced lengthwise
4 green onions, coarsely chopped
1/4 cup soy sauce
2 tablespoons water
2 tablespoons potato starch or cornstarch
Steamed basmati rce (page 129) to serve

In a pressure cooker, heat oils. Add onion and garlic and sauté 2 minutes. Add beef strips, stir well, and cook over high heat 1 minute. Stir in broth, sherry, brown sugar, salt, ginger root, and pepper flakes. Secure lid. Over high heat, develop steam to high pressure. Reduce heat to maintain pressure and cook 10 minutes. Release pressure according to manufacturer's directions. Remove lid.

Stir in tomatoes, bell pepper, and green onions. Secure lid. Over high heat, develop steam to medium-high pressure. Reduce heat to maintain pressure and cook 2 minutes. Release pressure according to manufacturer's directions. Remove lid.

Combine soy sauce, water, and potato starch in a small bowl. Blend until smooth. Gradually add to beef and vegetables, stirring gently until thickened and creamy. Serve beef and vegetables over steamed rice. Makes 6 servings.

Cook's Note: Partially freeze beef before cutting for more uniform strips.

Greek Meatballs & Spaghetti Sauce

This wonderful meat sauce has delicate Mediterranean flavors and can be made ahead and frozen up to two months.

Meatballs (see opposite)
1 large onion, minced
4 garlic cloves, crushed
2 slices bacon, diced
2 carrots, coarsely diced
1/3 cup chopped parsley
1 (29-oz.) can tomato sauce
1 cup beef broth or stock
2 tablespoons sherry
2 tablespoons light brown sugar
2 teaspoons salt
1/2 teaspoon crushed red pepper flakes
2 tablespoons dried oregano
1/2 teaspoon ground fennel

2 bay leaves
Cooked pasta or rice to serve

Meatballs:

1 pound lean ground beef, lamb, or turkey
1/4 cup sherry
1 egg, lightly beaten
1 medium-size onion, minced
2 garlic cloves, crushed
2 slices bread, finely crumbled
1 teaspoon salt
1/8 teaspoon freshly ground pepper
1/2 cup olive oil

Prepare meatballs. Set aside. In a pressure cooker, sauté onion, garlic, bacon, carrots, and parsley over medium-high heat 3 minutes. Add tomato sauce, broth, sherry, brown sugar, salt, pepper flakes, oregano, fennel, and bay leaves. Stir to combine, and add meatballs. Secure lid. Over medium-high heat, develop steam to high pressure. Reduce heat to maintain pressure and cook 10 minutes. Release pressure according to manufacturer's directions. Remove lid.

Gently stir meatballs and sauce. Discard bay leaves. Let stand 5 minutes. Skim fat from surface. Serve over pasta or rice. Makes 6 to 8 servings.

Meatballs

Combine beef, sherry, and egg in a bowl. Add onion, garlic, bread crumbs, salt, and pepper. Knead until completely mixed. Shape into walnut-size meatballs.

In a pressure cooker, sauté meatballs in hot oil over high heat until lightly browned. Cook about 10 meatballs at a time, turning with tongs.

Hearty Italian Meat Sauce

It's versatile, it's hearty, and it's delicious on pasta, rice, or vegetables.

1/4 cup olive oil
1 large onion, diced
4 garlic cloves, crushed
1 carrot, finely diced
1/4 pound prosciutto, diced
1 1/2 pounds ground beef chuck or ground
   turkey
1 pound Italian sausage with fennel, cut into
   2-inch pieces
2 cups beef broth
1 (29-oz.) can tomato sauce
2 tablespoons Marsala wine

1/2 cup diced green bell pepper
1/2 cup minced Italian parsley
2 tablespoons light brown sugar
1 1/2 teaspoons salt
1/2 teaspoon crushed red pepper flakes
1 tablespoon dried oregano
2 teaspoons dried basil
1 teaspoon dried rosemary
2 bay leaves

In a pressure cooker, heat oil. Add onion, garlic, carrot, and prosciutto and sauté in hot oil 3 minutes, stirring well. Add beef and cook 2 minutes, stirring to break up meat. Stir in sausage, broth, tomato sauce, wine, bell pepper, parsley, brown sugar, salt, pepper flakes, oregano, basil, rosemary, and bay leaves. Secure lid. Over high heat, develop steam to high pressure. Reduce heat to maintain pressure and cook 10 minutes. Release pressure according to manufacturer's directions. Remove lid.

  Stir sauce well. Discard bay leaves. Cook over medium-high heat, uncovered, 5 minutes to reduce liquid and intensify flavor. Let stand 5 minutes, then skim fat from surface. Makes about 10 servings.

Cook's Notes: I have layered this sauce with cooked ziti, Fontinella and Parmesan cheeses, and grilled eggplant, and baked it as a casserole. It's great!

  Sauce may be frozen in airtight containers up to 2 months. Thaw in refrigerator.

Hunter's Beef Onion Stew

A well-seasoned, robust peasant dish, this is juicy and satisfying on cold winter evenings.

1/4 cup olive oil
2 large onions, diced
4 garlic cloves, crushed
2 carrots, thinly sliced
2 slices bacon, diced
1 1/2 pounds beef round steak, cut into 2-inch cubes
1 (29-oz.) can Italian tomatoes, undrained
1 cup beef broth
1/2 cup chopped parsley

2 tablespoons light brown sugar
2 teaspoons salt
1/2 teaspoon pepper
3 tablespoons whole allspice in cheesecloth bag
4 medium-size potatoes, peeled and cut into eighths
2 1/2 pounds small pearl onions
2 tablespoons white wine vinegar
Crusty bread to serve

In a pressure cooker, heat oil. Add diced onions, garlic, carrots, and bacon and sauté in hot oil 3 minutes. Add beef, stir, and cook 1 minute. Stir in tomatoes, broth, parsley, brown sugar, salt, pepper, and allspice. Secure lid. Over high heat, develop steam to high pressure. Reduce heat to maintain pressure and cook 12 minutes. Release pressure according to manufacturer's directions. Remove lid.

Add potatoes, pearl onions, and vinegar. Stir gently to mix with beef. Secure lid. Over high heat, develop steam to high pressure. Reduce heat to maintain pressure and cook 6 minutes. Release pressure according to manufacturer's directions. Remove lid.

Stir stew gently. Remove allspice bag. Serve with hunks of crusty bread. Makes 6 servings.

Variation

Rabbit, cut into serving pieces, is frequently used in this stew instead of beef.

Mediterranean Beef Stew

Complete this hearty meal with hunks of Greek bread, feta cheese, and perhaps a tossed green salad.

1/4 cup olive oil
2 large white onions, sliced
3 garlic cloves, crushed
1 1/2 pounds stewing beef, cut into 2-inch cubes
1 (15-oz.) can tomato sauce
1 cup canned or fresh beef broth
2 bay leaves
1 tablespoon light brown sugar
2 cups (1 1/2-inch pieces) celery with leaves

2 carrots, cut into 2-inch pieces
4 potatoes, peeled and quartered
1/4 cup chopped parsley
2 teaspoons salt
1 teaspoon freshly ground pepper
2 1/2 teaspoons dried oregano
1 teaspoon dried rosemary
1 cup frozen whole-kernel corn
1 cup frozen green peas
2 tablespoons fresh lemon juice

In a pressure cooker, heat oil. Add onion and garlic and sauté in hot oil 3 minutes, stirring frequently. Add beef and cook 2 minutes, stirring occasionally. Stir in tomato sauce, broth, bay leaves, and brown sugar. Secure lid. Over high heat, develop steam to high pressure. Reduce heat to maintain pressure and cook 12 minutes. Release pressure according to manufacturer's directions. Remove lid.

Stir beef mixture. Add celery, carrots, potatoes, parsley, salt, pepper, oregano, and rosemary. Stir well. Secure lid. Over high heat, develop steam to medium-high pressure. Reduce heat to maintain pressure and cook 6 minutes. Release pressure according to manufacturer's directions. Remove lid.

Add corn, peas, and lemon juice to beef and vegetable mixture. Stir well. Cook 2 minutes, stirring occasionally. Discard bay leaves. Makes 6 servings.

Variation

Chicken pieces can be substituted for the beef. To reduce the fat, remove the skin from the chicken.

Sauerbraten

The sauce is rich and absolutely makes the dish!

1/4 cup olive oil
1 (3-lb.) beef sirloin roast
2 large onions, coarsely chopped
2 garlic cloves, crushed
1 carrot, coarsely chopped
1 celery stalk, coarsely chopped
2 cups beef broth
1 cup sweet red wine
1 1/2 teaspoons salt
1/2 teaspoon ground pepper

2 tablespoons bouquet garni (see page 191) plus 4 whole cloves in cheesecloth bag
2 bay leaves, broken in halves
6 potatoes, peeled and quartered
1/2 cup sour cream
1/4 cup butter, softened
1/4 cup tomato sauce
1/4 cup all-purpose flour

In a pressure cooker, heat oil. Add roast and brown in hot oil, turning to brown all sides. Remove and set aside.

Add onions, garlic, carrot, and celery and sauté in hot oil 3 minutes, scraping bottom of cooker with wooden spoon. Stir in broth, wine, salt, pepper, bouquet garni, and bay leaves. Add roast. Secure lid. Over high heat, develop steam to high pressure. Reduce heat to maintain pressure and cook 1 hour. Release pressure according to manufacturer's directions. Remove lid.

Transfer roast to a cutting board. Cover with foil to retain heat.

Strain cooking liquid, measure 2 cups, and pour into pressure cooker. Add potatoes. Secure lid. Over high heat, develop steam to high pressure. Reduce heat to maintain pressure and cook 5 minutes. Release pressure according to manufacturer's directions. Remove lid.

Using slotted spoon, transfer potatoes to a platter. Discard bay leaf halves and seasoning bag.

Combine sour cream, butter, tomato sauce, and flour in a small bowl, blending to paste consistency. Gradually add to cooking liquid and cook, stirring, 1 minute or until mixture is slightly thickened. Slice beef and arrange on platter with potatoes. Serve with sauce. Makes about 10 servings.

Cook's Note: Leftover beef makes marvelous hot sandwiches. It can be sliced and frozen up to 3 months. Thaw in refrigerator.

Short Ribs with Natural Gravy

Short ribs are taken from the beef chuck and traditionally cut into 3-inch pieces.
Short ribs are layers of fat and meat, which gives them a delicious juiciness.
To reduce the amount of fat in the dish, see Cook's Note below.

3 tablespoons prepared mustard
3 to 3 1/2 pounds beef short ribs (2 1/2 inch thick), excess fat trimmed
1/3 cup all-purpose flour
1/4 cup olive oil
4 leeks (white part only), sliced
1/3 cup chopped parsley
1 cup crushed canned tomatoes
1 1/2 cups beef broth
1/4 cup sherry

1 tablespoon brown sugar
1 1/2 teaspoons salt
1/2 teaspoon pepper
1 teaspoon dried tarragon
6 carrots, cut into 2-inch pieces
6 medium-size potatoes, peeled and cut into 1/2-inch slices
1/4 cup sour cream
1/4 cup butter, softened
1 1/2 tablespoons potato starch or flour

Brush mustard on surface of ribs. Place flour in a shallow dish. Coat ribs with flour, shaking to remove excess. In a pressure cooker, heat oil. Add ribs and sauté in hot oil, turning to brown on all sides. Remove and set aside.

Add leeks and parsley and sauté in hot oil 2 minutes. Stir in tomatoes, broth, sherry, brown sugar, salt, pepper, and tarragon. Add ribs. Secure lid. Over high heat, develop steam to high pressure. Reduce heat to maintain pressure and cook 18 minutes. Release pressure according to manufacturer's directions. Remove lid.

Add carrots and potatoes to rib mixture. Secure lid. Over high heat, develop steam to high pressure. Reduce heat to maintain pressure and cook 6 minutes. Release pressure according to manufacturer's directions. Remove lid.

Transfer ribs and vegetables to a platter. Combine sour cream, butter, and potato starch, blending until smooth. Gradually add to cooking liquid, stirring and cooking over medium heat 1 minute. Spoon sauce over ribs and vegetables. Makes about 8 servings.

Cook's Note: To skim off excess fat, drain meat through a colander after the first 18 minutes of cooking. Put juices in freezer 20 minutes. Fat will rise to surface. Skim fat off top. Return juices and meat to pressure cooker and continue to cook to completion.

Swiss Steak & Onions

Traditional in taste, but it's cooked in a fraction of the time.
Now you can even have this hearty dish midweek.

2 pounds beef round steak (1 1/2 inches thick)
1/2 cup seasoned bread crumbs
1/4 cup olive oil
1 medium-size onion, diced
2 garlic cloves, crushed
1 carrot, diced
1/4 cup minced parsley
1/2 teaspoon dried tarragon

1 bay leaf
2/3 cup beef broth
2 tablespoons light sherry
2 tablespoons tomato paste
5 large onions, sliced in rings
1 teaspoon salt
1/4 teaspoon pepper
Buttered noodles or steamed potatoes to serve

Cut steak into serving pieces, slitting edges to prevent curling. Place bread crumbs into a shallow dish. Coat steak pieces with bread crumbs, shaking to remove excess crumbs.

In a pressure cooker, heat oil. Add steak and sauté in hot oil, 2 pieces at a time to avoid crowding. Use long-handled tongs to turn steak to brown on both sides. Remove and set aside.

Add onion, garlic, carrot, parsley, tarragon, and bay leaf to hot oil and cook 3 minutes, stirring with wooden spoon to loosen browned particles on bottom of cooker. Stir in broth, sherry, and tomato paste. Mix well. Place steak pieces in sauce. Secure lid. Over high heat, develop steam to high pressure. Reduce heat to maintain pressure and cook 18 minutes. Release pressure according to manufacturer's directions. Remove lid.

Add onions to steak and sauce. Season with salt and pepper, stirring well. Secure lid. Over high heat, develop steam to high pressure. Reduce heat to maintain pressure and cook 2 minutes. Release pressure according to manufacturer's directions. Remove lid.

Gently stir beef and sauce with wooden spoon. Discard bay leaf. Serve with noodles or potatoes. Makes 6 to 8 servings.

Cook's Note: Buy bottom round steak. It is firm, lean, and well flavored. The pressure cooker tenderizes this cut very nicely.

Greek Lamb & Bean Stew

A favorite dish in Greek restaurants and homes, this fresh bean stew is robust in flavor. The beans are supposed to be well cooked, so don't expect crunchy beans!

1/4 cup olive oil
2 large white onions, sliced
3 garlic cloves, crushed
2 pounds lamb shoulder, trimmed of fat and
    cut into 2-inch cubes
1/4 cup all-purpose flour
1 (29-oz.) can Italian plum tomatoes
2 tablespoons tomato paste
1/4 cup chopped parsley
2 tablespoons brown sugar

2 teaspoons sea salt or granulated salt
1/2 teaspoon freshly ground black pepper
2 tablespoons dried spearmint
2 tablespoons dried dill weed
1 teaspoon dried oregano
1 1/2 pounds green beans, ends removed and
    cut into 2-inch pieces
3 potatoes, peeled and quartered
Crusty bread to serve

In a large pressure cooker, heat oil. Add onions and garlic and sauté in oil 2 minutes. Dust lamb pieces with flour, add to onion and garlic, and sauté 2 minutes, stirring occasionally. Stir in tomatoes, tomato paste, parsley, brown sugar, salt, pepper, spearmint, dill, and oregano. Secure lid. Over high heat, develop steam to high pressure. Reduce heat to maintain pressure and cook 8 minutes. Release pressure according to manufacturer's directions. Remove lid.

  Stir lamb and sauce. Add green beans and potatoes. Stir well. Secure lid. Over high heat, develop steam to high pressure. Reduce heat to maintain pressure and cook 8 minutes. Release pressure according to manufacturer's directions. Remove lid.

  Stir stew. Cook over high heat 3 minutes, stirring occasionally, to reduce liquid and intensify flavor. Serve with crusty bread. Makes 6 servings.

Stuffed Head of Cabbage

What a beautiful presentation this dish makes. Everyone oohs and aahs when served.

1 (2 1/2-lb.) head green cabbage
1/4 cup olive oil or butter
2 large onions, diced
2 garlic cloves, crushed
1/3 cup minced parsley
1 carrot, diced
2 celery stalks, chopped
1 pound ground beef, lamb, or turkey
1 cup long-grain white rice
2 cups beef or chicken broth
1/3 cup canned chopped tomatoes, undrained
1 teaspoon sugar
1 teaspoon salt
1/2 teaspoon pepper

2 tablespoons dried dill weed
1 teaspoon dried thyme

Tomato Sauce:

1/4 cup olive oil
1 onion, sliced
2 garlic cloves, crushed
1/2 green bell pepper, diced
2 cups beef or chicken stock
1 cup canned chopped tomatoes, undrained
1 tablespoon brown sugar
1 teaspoon salt
1/2 teaspoon black pepper
2 teaspoons dried oregano

Using a grapefruit knife or paring knife, hollow out center of cabbage head. Begin by cutting out core, removing center leaves as they are loosened. Remove leaves until outer leaves form a 2-inch-thick shell. Set aside.

In a pressure cooker, heat oil. Add onions, garlic, parsley, carrot, and celery and sauté in hot oil 3 minutes. Crumble meat into mixture and stir well. Stir in rice, broth, tomatoes, sugar, salt, pepper, dill, and thyme. Mix thoroughly. Secure lid. Over high heat, develop steam to high pressure. Reduce heat to maintain pressure and cook 6 minutes. Release pressure according to manufacturer's directions. Remove lid.

Stir meat and rice mixture thoroughly. Spoon into cabbage shell, mounding at top. Wrap a 24-inch length of cheesecloth around cabbage, overlapping at top. Set aside.

Rinse the pressure cooker and wipe dry. Prepare sauce in pressure cooker.

Place steamer basket over sauce in cooker. Place cabbage in steamer basket. Secure lid. Over high heat, develop steam to high pressure. Reduce heat to maintain pressure and cook 10 minutes. Release pressure according to manufacturer's directions. Remove lid.

Carefully transfer the stuffed cabbage to a serving platter. Unwrap cheesecloth and slip from beneath cabbage. Ladle sauce over top of cabbage and around platter. Cut cabbage into wedges to serve. Makes 6 to 8 servings.

Tomato Sauce

In pressure cooker, heat oil. Add onion, garlic, and bell pepper and sauté in hot oil 2 minutes. Stir in broth, tomatoes, brown sugar, salt, black pepper, and oregano. Stir well.

Sloppy Joes with Peppers

Fun time recipe! These juicy, lightly spiced sloppy joes will be a favorite with everyone young at heart.

2 slices bacon, diced into small pieces
2 tablespoons olive oil
1 large onion, diced
2 garlic cloves, crushed
1 pound lean ground beef or ground turkey
1 green bell pepper, sliced
1/2 cup beef broth
1/4 cup tomato paste

2 tablespoons light brown sugar
1 teaspoon salt
1/4 teaspoon crushed red pepper flakes
1/2 teaspoon chili powder
2 teaspoons prepared mustard
1 tablespoon Worcestershire sauce
8 crusty rolls or hamburger buns, warmed, to serve

In a pressure cooker, sauté bacon until crisp. Add oil, onion, and garlic and sauté 3 minutes. Add beef and cook 2 minutes, stirring to break up meat. Add bell pepper, broth, tomato paste, brown sugar, salt, pepper flakes, chili powder, mustard, and Worcestershire sauce. Stir well. Secure lid. Over medium-high heat, develop steam to medium pressure. Reduce heat to maintain pressure and cook 6 minutes. Release pressure according to manufacturer's directions. Remove lid.

Stir beef mixture thoroughly. Serve on rolls or buns. Makes 6 servings.

Irish Stew

This traditional stew is always a composite of root vegetables and lamb or mutton.
Since mutton is much stronger in flavor than the young lamb, most recipes use lamb. The flavors
of the stew are fabulous, and it is traditionally served with dumplings.

1/4 cup corn oil or olive oil
2 pounds lamb shoulder, cut into 2-inch cubes
3 large onions, thinly sliced
1/3 cup minced parsley
2 cups beef broth
1 tablespoon tomato paste
1 1/2 teaspoons salt
1/4 teaspoon pepper
2 bay leaves

6 celery stalks, cut into 2-inch pieces
6 small carrots, cut into 2-inch pieces
6 medium-size potatoes, peeled and cut into
   sixths
2 medium-size turnips, peeled and cut into
   1/4-inch slices
1/4 cup butter, softened
1 1/2 tablespoons potato starch or flour
Dumplings to serve (optional)

In a pressure cooker, heat oil. Add lamb pieces and sauté in hot oil, turning with long-handled tongs to brown on both sides. Remove lamb and set aside. Add onions and parsley and sauté in hot oil 2 minutes. Stir in broth, tomato paste, salt, pepper, and bay leaves. Stir well. Add lamb. Secure lid. Over high heat, develop steam to high pressure. Reduce heat to maintain pressure and cook 8 minutes. Release pressure according to manufacturer's directions. Remove lid.

  Stir lamb and liquid. Stir in celery, carrots, potatoes, and turnips. Secure lid. Over high heat, develop steam to medium pressure. Reduce heat to maintain pressure and cook 6 minutes. Release pressure according to manufacturer's directions. Remove lid.

  Remove bay leaf. Combine butter and starch, blending to paste consistency. Stir into lamb and vegetables and cook over medium-high heat 1 minute.

  Serve over dumplings, if desired. Makes 6 servings.

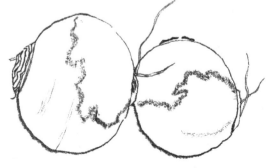

Italian Country Lamb & White Bean Stew

This country stew, full of the flavors of old Italy, is a perfect meal for supper on a cold night.

2 cups dried white beans
1/3 cup olive oil
1/4 pound pancetta or bacon, diced
2 large onions, diced
2 carrots, cut into 1/2-inch slices
3 garlic cloves, crushed
1/2 cup minced parsley
2 pounds lamb shoulder, trimmed of fat and
  cut into 2-inch cubes
1 (15-oz.) can crushed tomatoes, undrained
1 large green bell pepper, diced

3 cups chicken broth
2 tablespoons sherry
2 tablespoons brown sugar
2 teaspoons salt
1 teaspoon crushed red pepper flakes
2 teaspoons dried basil
2 teaspoons dried oregano
2 bay leaves
1/2 cup (2 ounces) grated Parmesan cheese
Italian bread to serve

Place beans in a bowl with enough water to cover by 2 inches. Soak overnight. Drain.

In a pressure cooker, heat oil. Add pancetta and sauté in hot oil 1 minute. Stir in onions, carrots, garlic, and parsley. Sauté 2 minutes. Add lamb, tomatoes, bell pepper, beans, broth, sherry, brown sugar, salt, pepper flakes, basil, oregano, and bay leaves. Stir well. Secure lid. Over high heat, develop steam to high pressure. Reduce heat to maintain pressure and cook 18 minutes. Release pressure according to manufacturer's directions. Remove lid.

Stir stew and discard bay leaves. Transfer to a serving platter and sprinkle with cheese.

Serve with large hunks of Italian bread. Makes 6 to 8 servings.

Cook's Note: Lamb is readily available in the meat department of supermarkets. Baby lamb is 6 to 8 weeks old, spring lamb 3 to 5 months old, and beyond that up to 1 year old, it is referred to as lamb. Mutton is more than 1 year old.

Lamb Shanks in Mustard Sauce

The shank is an extremely flavorful cut of meat. It comes from the front leg of the animal and requires long periods of conventional cooking. This is when the pressure cooker excels; it cuts the cooking time by two-thirds without reducing the flavor of the dish.

---

2 teaspoons salt
1/2 teaspoon pepper
1/3 cup prepared mustard
6 lamb shanks, split in halves
1/2 cup seasoned bread crumbs
1/3 cup olive oil
4 leeks (white part only), thinly sliced

3 garlic cloves, crushed
2 tablespoons sherry
1 cup beef broth
2 teaspoons tomato paste
1/3 cup half-and-half, cream, or drained low-fat yogurt
1 1/2 tablespoons potato starch or flour
Steamed rice and vegetables to serve

Combine salt, pepper, and mustard in a small bowl. Brush mixture over lamb pieces. Roll in bread crumbs, shaking to remove excess crumbs.

In a pressure cooker, heat oil. Add lamb pieces and sauté in hot oil, using long-handled tongs to turn to brown on all sides. Transfer lamb to a platter and reserve.

Add leeks and garlic and sauté in hot oil over medium heat 2 minutes. Add sherry and stir well. Stir in broth, tomato paste, and remaining mustard mixture. Stir well. Add lamb pieces. Secure lid. Over high heat, develop steam to high pressure. Reduce heat to maintain pressure and cook 20 minutes. Release pressure according to manufacturer's directions. Remove lid.

Transfer lamb pieces to a platter and cover to retain heat.

Combine half-and-half and potato starch, blending until smooth. Gradually add to cooking liquid and cook over medium heat 1 minute, stirring slowly. Spoon sauce over lamb. Serve with rice and vegetables. Makes 6 servings.

Lamb Shanks with Orzo, Greek Village Style

Orzo is a tiny pasta resembling rice in shape and with a satisfying, full-bodied texture.

1/4 cup olive oil
4 lamb shanks, split in halves
2 large onions, diced
3 garlic cloves, crushed
1/2 cup chopped parsley
4 1/2 cups beef broth
1/2 cup tomato sauce
2 tablespoons light sherry

2 tablespoons light brown sugar
1 1/2 teaspoons salt
1/2 teaspoon crushed red pepper flakes
2 teaspoons dried oregano
1 teaspoon dried rosemary
1/2 teaspoon ground fennel
2 bay leaves
1 1/2 cups orzo
Greek bread and feta cheese to serve

In a pressure cooker, heat oil. Add lamb pieces and sauté in hot oil, using long-handled tongs to turn to brown on all sides. Transfer lamb to a platter; reserve.

Add onions, garlic, and parsley and sauté in hot oil 3 minutes. Stir in broth, tomato sauce, sherry, brown sugar, salt, pepper flakes, oregano, rosemary, fennel, and bay leaves. Add lamb shanks. Secure lid. Over high heat, develop steam to high pressure. Reduce heat to maintain pressure and cook 10 minutes. Release pressure according to manufacturer's directions. Remove lid.

Stir orzo into lamb and sauce. Secure lid. Over high heat, develop steam to high pressure. Insert a heat diffuser between pan and heat. Reduce heat to maintain pressure and cook 10 minutes. Release pressure according to manufacturer's directions. Remove lid.

Stir lamb mixture thoroughly and discard bay leaves. Transfer to a large platter and serve with Greek bread and feta cheese. Makes 6 servings.

Cook's Note: Have the butcher split the lamb shanks in half. This will allow the delicious marrow to be released during cooking, adding fabulous flavor to the dish.

Shepherd's Pie

Shepherd's Pie was originally developed in England as an economical way to use leftovers. Therefore, if you have cooked lamb, substitute it for the ground lamb and cut the cooking time to 3 minutes.

3 slices bacon, cut into 1-inch pieces
2 tablespoons olive oil
1 large onion, diced
3 garlic cloves, crushed
1/3 cup minced parsley
1 pound ground lamb
1/2 cup beef broth
1/2 cup tomato sauce
3 carrots, cut into 1-inch pieces
1 1/2 cups (1-inch pieces) celery
1/2 green bell pepper, diced
2 tablespoons sherry
1 1/2 teaspoons salt
1/2 teaspoon black pepper

1 teaspoon dried basil
1 teaspoon dried oregano
1/2 teaspoon dried rosemary
2 bay leaves
1 cup frozen green peas
Potato Topping (see below)

Potato Topping:

1 cup water
5 medium-size potatoes, peeled and cut into
    1/2-inch cubes
3/4 teaspoon salt
1/4 teaspoon white pepper
1/4 cup sour cream
1/3 cup freshly grated Parmesan cheese

In a pressure cooker, sauté bacon 2 minutes until crisp. Stir in oil. Add onion, garlic, and parsley and sauté 3 minutes. Crumble lamb into mixture and stir with wooden spoon. Add broth, tomato sauce, carrots, celery, bell pepper, sherry, salt, black pepper, basil, oregano, rosemary, and bay leaves. Stir well. Secure lid. Over high heat, develop steam to high pressure. Reduce heat to maintain pressure and cook 8 minutes. Release pressure according to manufacturer's directions. Remove lid.

Skim surface to remove excess grease. Stir in peas. Cook over high heat 2 minutes, stirring occasionally. Remove bay leaves. Ladle mixture into a 13" x 9" baking dish. Prepare Potato Topping.

Preheat broiler. Press potatoes through pastry tube in an artistic pattern on top of lamb mixture. Sprinkle with remaining cheese. Broil a couple of minutes until golden brown. Makes 6 to 8 servings.

Potato Topping

Pour water into pressure cooker. Place potatoes in steam basket and insert in cooker. Secure lid. Over high heat, develop steam to high pressure. Reduce heat to maintain pressure and cook 5 minutes.

Release pressure according to manufacturer's directions. Remove lid.

Remove basket and drain potatoes. Transfer to a bowl. Sprinkle with salt and pepper. Using an electric mixer, whip potatoes on low speed until mashed. Add sour cream, 1 tablespoon at a time, and continue to whip. Add 1/4 cup of the cheese and whip until smooth and fluffy. Spoon potatoes into a 16-inch pastry bag fitted with a number 5 or 6 star pastry tube.

Rice Meatballs in Egg-Lemon Sauce

This lemon-sauced dish is traditionally made with ground lamb but ground turkey can be used.

1 1/2 pounds ground lamb
1 medium-size onion, diced
2 garlic cloves, crushed
1 cup long-grain white rice
1 1/2 teaspoons salt
1/4 teaspoon freshly ground pepper
1 teaspoon dried oregano
1/3 cup olive oil
3 cups beef or chicken broth

1 teaspoon dried dill weed
Egg-Lemon Sauce (see below)
Steamed green beans or broccoli to serve

Egg-Lemon Sauce:
3 large eggs, at room temperature
1 tablespoon cornstarch
1/3 cup fresh lemon juice

Combine lamb, onion, garlic, rice, salt, pepper, and oregano in a bowl. Mix until thoroughly blended. Shape mixture into walnut-size balls.

In a pressure cooker, heat oil. Add meatballs and sauté in hot oil 2 minutes, using long-handled tongs to turn to brown on all sides. Stir in broth and dill. Secure lid. Over high heat, develop steam to high pressure. Reduce heat to maintain pressure and cook 10 minutes. Release pressure according to manufacturer's directions. Remove lid.

Prepare sauce. Slowly pour sauce over meatballs, stirring gently to mix. Serve with green beans or broccoli. Makes 6 servings.

Egg-Lemon Sauce
Using an electric mixer, beat eggs and cornstarch on medium-high speed 5 minutes. Gradually add lemon juice, continuing to beat. Gradually add 1/3 cup cooking liquid from meatballs.

German Pork Chops & Sauerkraut

Caraway seeds lend a wonderful nutty flavor to this traditional German dish.
The caraway seeds are aromatic and come from the parsley family.

6 pork chops (1 inch thick)
1/3 cup all-purpose flour
3 slices bacon, cut into 1-inch pieces
1/4 cup butter or 1/4 cup olive oil
2 large onions, sliced
4 garlic cloves, crushed
3 carrots, cut into 1/2-inch slices
1 cup apple juice
1 cup chicken broth
1 tablespoon fresh lemon juice

1 1/4 teaspoons salt
1/2 teaspoon pepper
1 teaspoon dried thyme
2 bay leaves
8 juniper berries and 1 tablespoon caraway
   seeds in cheesecloth bag
2 (16-oz.) jars sauerkraut, drained and rinsed
2 teaspoons potato starch or flour
Steamed Whole Potatoes (page 154) to serve

Dust pork chops with flour, shaking to remove excess.

In a pressure cooker, sauté bacon 2 minutes until crisp. Add butter and stir until melted and foaming. Add pork chops and sauté over medium heat until browned on both sides, turning with long-handled tongs. Transfer pork chops to a platter and reserve.

Add onions, garlic, and carrots and sauté 1 minute. Stir in apple juice, broth, lemon juice, salt, pepper, thyme, bay leaves, and juniper berries and caraway seeds. Stir well. Add pork chops. Secure lid. Over high heat, develop steam to high pressure. Reduce heat to maintain pressure and cook 15 minutes. Release pressure according to manufacturer's directions. Remove lid.

Stir sauerkraut into pork chop mixture and cook over high heat 3 minutes. Discard cheesecloth bag and bay leaves. Mix potato starch with 1/4 cup juices and pour into hot mixture. Cook, stirring, over medium heat 1 minute. Serve hot. Serve with potatoes. Makes 6 servings.

Saucy Herbed Pork Chops

Today's pork is leaner in fat and higher in protein than in years past. Thanks to improved techniques of feeding and growing, today's pork has at least one-third fewer calories than in the past.

6 pork chops (1 inch thick)
1/3 cup all-purpose flour
1/3 cup olive oil
1 large onion, sliced
2 garlic cloves, crushed
1/4 cup chopped parsley
1 (15-oz.) can crushed tomatoes, undrained
1 cup chicken broth

2 tablespoons brown sugar
1 1/2 teaspoons salt
1/2 teaspoon crushed red pepper flakes
1 1/2 teaspoons dried thyme
1 teaspoon ground fennel
2 tablespoons milk or half-and-half
2 tablespoons potato starch or flour
Cooked noodles (page 130) or rice (page 129) to serve

Dust pork chops with flour, shaking to remove excess flour. In a pressure cooker, heat oil. Add chops, 2 at a time, and sauté in hot oil until browned on both sides. Transfer pork chops to a platter; reserve.

Add onion, garlic, and parsley and sauté in hot oil 2 minutes, stirring well and scraping bottom of pan. Stir in tomatoes, broth, brown sugar, salt, pepper flakes, thyme, and fennel. Add pork chops. Secure lid. Over high heat, develop steam to high pressure. Reduce heat to maintain pressure and cook 14 minutes. Release pressure according to manufacturer's directions. Remove lid.

Continue cooking over medium heat while blending milk and potato starch in a small bowl. Using tongs, transfer pork chops to a serving platter. Whisk starch mixture into tomato mixture and cook, stirring, 1 minute. Spoon sauce over the pork chops. Serve with noodles or rice. Makes 6 servings.

Cook's Note: Pressure cooking prevents any problem with trichinosis in pork, because the internal temperature of the meat goes beyond 137°F (60°C), which is needed to destroy the organism.

Stuffed Veal Bundles with Leek Sauce

The leeks add a delicate sweetness to the sauce.

6 veal cutlets
3 slices bread
1/8 cup milk or chicken broth
1/2 pound bulk breakfast sausage
1 shallot, minced
3 tablespoons chopped parsley
1 cup seasoned bread crumbs
1/3 cup olive oil
Sauce (see opposite)
3 tablespoons butter, softened
1/4 cup half-and-half
3 tablespoons all-purpose flour
Lemon slices to garnish
Rice and a vegetable to serve

Sauce:

4 leeks (white part only), thinly sliced
1/2 cup chicken broth
1/2 cup white wine
2 tablespoons sherry
1 tablespoon fresh lemon juice
1 teaspoon salt
1/4 teaspoon white pepper
1/2 teaspoon dried tarragon
1 bay leaf

Using a meat mallet, flatten cutlets between two sheets of waxed paper or plastic wrap until thin and rectangular in shape.

Soak bread in milk, drain, and crumble. Combine with sausage, shallot, and parsley in a bowl. Mix thoroughly. Place 1/4 cup stuffing on each cutlet and fold edges, envelope style, to enclose stuffing. Secure with cotton twine and roll bundles in bread crumbs.

In a pressure cooker, heat oil. Add bundles and sauté in hot oil, using long-handled tongs to turn to brown on all sides. Remove and set aside. Prepare sauce in pressure cooker.

Place veal bundles in sauce. Secure lid. Over high heat, develop steam to high pressure. Reduce heat to maintain pressure and cook 10 minutes. Release pressure according to manufacturer's directions. Remove lid.

Place bundles on a platter. Snip string and remove from bundles. Cover bundles with foil to retain heat.

Strain cooking liquid through a fine sieve and return to cooker. Combine butter, half-and-half, and flour in a small bowl, blending to paste consistency. Stir paste into cooking liquid over medium-high heat and cook, stirring, until mixture begins to thicken, about 1 minute. Spoon sauce over veal bundles and garnish with lemon slices. Serve with rice and a vegetable. Makes 6 servings.

Sauce
Add leeks to pressure cooker and sauté in oil over medium heat 2 minutes, scraping bottom with a wooden spoon. Add broth, wine, sherry, lemon juice, salt, pepper, tarragon, and bay leaf. Stir well.

Cook's Note: Leeks grow in sandy soil and are full of grit. Before slicing the leeks, remove green tops, cut lengthwise almost to the center, and rinse very well under cool, running water.

Greek Pork Chops with Potatoes & Peas

Look for light pink flesh when selecting pork cuts. The darker the flesh, the older the animal.

6 pork chops (1 inch thick)
1/3 cup seasoned bread crumbs
1/4 cup olive oil
3 large onions, sliced
3 garlic cloves, crushed
2 cups chicken broth
3 tablespoons tomato paste

1 1/4 teaspoons salt
1/4 teaspoon pepper
2 teaspoons dried oregano
1 bay leaf
6 medium-size potatoes, peeled and cut into sixths
2 cups frozen green peas
Greek bread and feta cheese to serve

Coat both sides of pork chops with bread crumbs. In a pressure cooker, heat oil. Add pork chops, 2 at a time, and sauté in hot oil until browned on both sides. Transfer to a platter; reserve.

Add onions and garlic and sauté in hot oil 3 minutes, stirring and scraping bottom of pan. Stir in broth, tomato paste, salt, pepper, oregano, and bay leaf. Stir well. Place pork chops in sauce. Secure lid. Over high heat, develop steam to high pressure. Reduce heat to maintain pressure and cook 8 minutes. Release pressure according to manufacturer's directions. Remove lid.

Add potatoes to pork chops. Secure lid. Over high heat, develop steam to high pressure. Reduce heat to maintain pressure and cook 5 minutes. Release pressure according to manufacturer's directions. Remove lid.

Stir peas into pork chop and potato mixture. Cook over medium heat 2 minutes. Serve with hunks of Greek bread and feta cheese. Makes 6 servings.

Veal Florentine with Parmesan

This Venetian recipe is full of great, healthy flavors.

2 pounds veal steak
1/3 cup bread crumbs
2 tablespoons butter
1/4 cup corn oil or olive oil
3 tablespoons thinly sliced shallots
1 tablespoon sherry
1 cup chicken broth

2 tablespoons fresh lemon juice
1 teaspoon dried tarragon
1 bay leaf
2 (10-oz.) packages fresh spinach, rinsed well
1/3 cup grated Parmesan cheese
Steamed rice (page 129) or potatoes (page 154) to serve

Cut veal into 6 pieces. Using a meat mallet, flatten cutlets between two sheets of waxed paper or plastic wrap to 1/4-inch thickness. Press bread crumbs on both sides of veal, shaking to remove excess crumbs.

In a pressure cooker, heat butter and oil. Add veal and sauté until lightly browned on both sides, turning with long-handled tongs. Remove and set aside. Add shallots and sauté 1 minute, scraping the bottom of the cooker to release browned veal particles. Stir in sherry. Add broth, lemon juice, tarragon, and bay leaf. Stir well. Place veal in sauce. Secure lid. Over high heat, develop steam to high pressure. Reduce heat to maintain pressure and cook 10 minutes. Release pressure according to manufacturer's directions. Remove lid.

Place veal on a platter and cover to retain heat.

Add spinach to cooking liquid. Over high heat, develop steam to medium pressure. Reduce heat to maintain pressure and cook 3 minutes. Release pressure according to manufacturer's directions. Remove lid.

Stir spinach thoroughly. Drain through a colander, using a large, flat spatula to press excess moisture from spinach. Discard bay leaf. Spoon a serving of spinach on each serving plate and top with a veal cutlet. Sprinkle with cheese. Serve with rice or potatoes. Makes 6 servings.

Cook's Note: Veal refers to a young calf up to 3 months old that is milk-fed. The flesh is generally pinkish white and very tender when prepared properly.

Veal Paprika with Spaetzle Noodles

The butcher will cut the veal into pieces upon request. Ask for a blade cut or arm steak.
The bone will add extra flavor to this Hungarian favorite.

1/4 cup olive oil
2 onions, sliced
1 garlic clove, crushed
1/4 cup finely diced carrot
1 1/2 pounds stewing veal, cut into 1-inch cubes
2 cups chicken broth
2 tablespoons sherry
2 tablespoons tomato paste
1/4 cup chopped parsley
1 teaspoon salt

1/4 teaspoon white pepper
1 tablespoon paprika
1 teaspoon dried thyme
1 teaspoon caraway seeds in cheesecloth bag
1 bay leaf
1/2 cup sour cream
2 tablespoons butter, softened
2 tablespoons all-purpose flour
Cooked spaetzle or cavatelli pasta to serve

In pressure cooker, heat oil. Add onions, garlic, and carrot and sauté in hot oil over medium-high heat 3 minutes. Add veal and cook over high heat 1 minute, stirring frequently. Stir in broth, sherry, tomato paste, parsley, salt, pepper, paprika, thyme, caraway seeds, and bay leaf. Secure lid. Over high heat, develop steam to high pressure. Reduce heat to maintain pressure and cook 10 minutes. Release pressure according to manufacturer's directions. Remove lid.

Discard bay leaf and caraway seeds. Stir veal mixture well. Combine sour cream, butter, and flour in a small bowl, blending to paste consistency. Add, 1 tablespoon at a time, to veal mixture and cook, stirring, until thoroughly blended and mixture begins to thicken.

Serve over spaetzle or pasta. Makes 6 servings.

Veal Piccata with Shrimp

Veal steak comes from the leg of the animal. It is generally pink in color with some marbling.
Your butcher will be happy to slice this into pieces for you.

1 1/2 pounds veal steak, trimmed of fat and
  bone removed
1/3 cup seasoned bread crumbs
2 tablespoons butter
2 tablespoons olive oil
4 shallots, finely diced
3 garlic cloves, crushed
1 teaspoon dried basil
3/4 cup chicken broth
1/3 cup fresh lemon juice

1 tablespoon sherry
2 teaspoons salt
1/4 teaspoon white pepper
12 large shrimp, shelled and deveined
1 cup pitted ripe olives, coarsely chopped
1/4 cup sour cream
1 tablespoon potato starch or flour
1/4 cup grated Parmesan cheese
Steamed rice and a green vegetable to serve

Cut veal into 6 serving pieces. Using meat mallet, flatten between two pieces of waxed paper or plastic wrap to 1/2-inch thickness. Press bread crumbs into both sides of veal, shaking to remove excess crumbs.

In a pressure cooker, heat butter and oil. Add veal and sauté, using long-handled tongs to turn to brown on both sides. Remove and set aside.

Add shallots and garlic and sauté 1 minute, stirring and scraping the bottom of the cooker to dislodge browned particles. Sprinkle with basil and stir. Add broth, lemon juice, sherry, salt, and pepper. Mix well. Add veal. Secure lid. Over high heat, develop steam to high pressure. Reduce heat to maintain pressure and cook 10 minutes. Release pressure according to manufacturer's directions. Remove lid.

Add shrimp and olives to veal. Cook over high heat 3 minutes. Transfer veal to a platter. Top each portion with 2 shrimp.

Combine sour cream and potato starch in a small bowl. Stir into cooking liquid. Cook, stirring, over medium heat 1 minute. Spoon sauce over veal and shrimp. Sprinkle with cheese. Serve with rice and a green vegetable. Makes 6 servings.

Veal Steak with Herbed Leeks & Cognac

When selecting veal, let color be your guide. The flesh should be light pink with a grayish white tinge.
If it appears to be more on the red side, the animal could be over four months old
and should not be considered or sold as veal.

2 pounds veal steak (1 inch thick)
1/2 cup seasoned bread crumbs
1/3 cup olive oil
2 leeks (white part only), thinly sliced
2 garlic cloves, crushed
1/2 cup minced parsley
3/4 cup beef broth
1/4 cup cognac, brandy, or bourbon
1/4 cup tomato sauce
1 teaspoon sugar
1 teaspoon salt

1/4 teaspoon white pepper
1 teaspoon dried tarragon
1 bay leaf
1/2 teaspoon lemon zest
8 leeks (white part only), sliced into rings
3 tablespoons butter, softened
2 tablespoons sour cream
1 teaspoon potato starch or flour
Steamed Whole Potatoes (page 154) to serve

Cut veal into 6 serving pieces. Press bread crumbs into both sides of veal. In a pressure cooker, heat oil. Add veal and sauté in hot oil, using long-handled tongs to turn to brown on both sides. Remove veal and set aside.

Add 2 thinly sliced leeks, garlic, and parsley and sauté in hot oil 3 minutes, scraping bottom to loosen browned particles. Add broth, cognac, tomato sauce, sugar, salt, pepper, tarragon, bay leaf, and lemon zest. Stir well. Add veal. Secure lid. Over high heat, develop steam to high pressure. Reduce heat to maintain pressure and cook 10 minutes. Release pressure according to manufacturer's directions. Remove lid.

Stir veal and cooking liquid. Add sliced leeks. Secure lid. Over high heat, develop steam to medium-high pressure. Reduce heat to maintain pressure and cook 2 minutes. Release pressure according to manufacturer's directions. Remove lid.

Remove veal and place on a platter. Cover to retain heat. Discard bay leaf.

Combine butter, sour cream, and potato starch in a small bowl, blending to paste consistency. Stir into cooking liquid and cook, stirring, over medium heat until sauce begins to thicken, about 1 minute.

Spoon leek rings and sauce over veal. Serve with potatoes. Makes 6 servings.

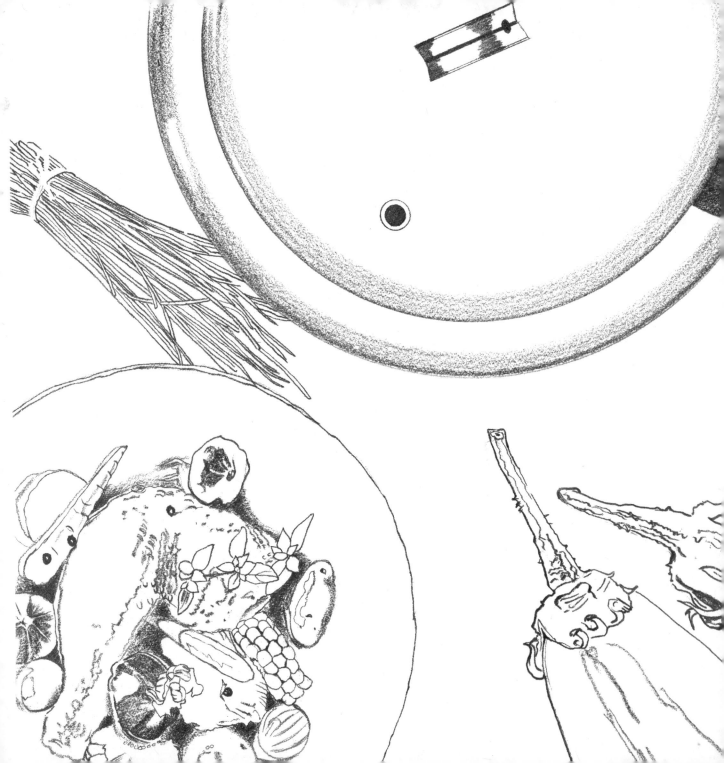

Poultry

Poultry blends well with other ingredients when cooked. It is excellent when cooked in the pressure cooker.

It is very economical to purchase a whole chicken, duck, or turkey and cut it into pieces. The skin can be removed, if desired. The pieces may be used in stocks, stews, or any favorite recipe. Remaining pieces may be wrapped airtight in freezer paper, marked with the item and date, and frozen for future use.

Some people prefer free-range poultry because of its richer, purer flavor. It can be found in most butcher shops. If you live in an area where kosher or Amish birds are available, they are excellent in quality and flavor.

BUYING POULTRY

When buying poultry, be selective. Look for a fresh, moist surface with a rich pink and yellow hue. Dark gray dry marks on the bird indicate it was improperly frozen and handled and that bacteria may be present. Look for a meaty bird without skin tears or bruises.

Poultry is available in these categories:

- **Fryer:** Tender and great for any kind of preparation, including barbecuing.
- **Broiler:** Firmer than a fryer but still tender.
- **Roaster:** A more mature, tougher bird best used for stuffing and roasting.

COOKING TIME FOR POULTRY

Cut poultry into uniform pieces before cooking in the pressure cooker to ensure even cooking.

Cook poultry 10 minutes for each 2 inches of thickness.

Chicken Cavatelli with Fontinella

Cavatelli is a thick, rolled pasta found in Italian food stores. It has a wonderful, satisfying texture.

1/4 cup olive oil
1 (2 1/2-lb.) chicken, cut into 8 pieces (2 inches thick)
1 large white onion, chopped
2 garlic cloves, crushed
3 1/2 cups chicken broth or stock
1 (15-oz.) can tomato puree
1 (16-oz.) package cavatelli pasta
1 teaspoon brown sugar

2 teaspoons salt
1/4 teaspoon freshly ground pepper
1 1/2 teaspoons dried oregano, crushed between palms
1 teaspoon dried rosemary, crushed between palms
1 bay leaf
1 cup (4 ounces) grated Fontinella cheese

In a pressure cooker, heat oil. Add chicken pieces and brown in hot oil, using long-handled tongs to turn. Remove with tongs and set aside. Add onion and garlic and sauté in hot oil over medium heat about 3 minutes. Stir in broth, tomato puree, pasta, brown sugar, salt, pepper, oregano, rosemary, and bay leaf. Secure lid. Over high heat, develop steam to high pressure; slide a heat diffuser over burner. Reduce heat to maintain pressure and cook 18 minutes. Release pressure according to manufacturer's directions. Remove lid. Remove diffuser.

Stir pasta mixture. Using tongs, add reserved chicken pieces. Secure lid. Over high heat, develop steam to medium-high pressure, add heat diffuser, and cook 10 minutes. Release pressure according to manufacturer's directions. Remove lid.

Discard bay leaf. Place chicken and pasta on large platter and sprinkle with cheese. Toss gently to mix. Makes 6 servings.

Cook's Note: This dish can also be prepared using other pastas; however, timing charts should be referred to for perfect results.

Chicken-Broccoli Bundles

Serve steamed rice with this delicious and colorful dish.

Broccoli Filling (see opposite)
6 chicken breast halves, skin removed and
    boned
1/4 cup plus 2 tablespoons olive oil, divided
1 garlic clove, crushed
1 1/4 teaspoons salt, divided
About 1/8 teaspoon pepper plus a dash,
    divided
1 1/2 pounds broccoli (about 3 heads)
1/3 cup seasoned bread crumbs
1 tablespoon all-purpose flour

1 cup chicken broth
Steamed rice to serve

Broccoli Filling:
1/2 pound broccoli (1 small head)
3 tablespoons olive oil
1 green onion, minced
1 teaspoon fresh lemon juice
1/4 cup grated Asiago or Kaseri cheese

Prepare filling. Using a meat mallet, gently flatten chicken pieces to 1/4 inch thick. Combine 2 tablespoons oil, garlic, 1/4 teaspoon salt, and a dash of pepper in a small bowl. Rub mixture over chicken surface. Peel broccoli stalks. Cut each head into 6 portions.

Mound 1/4 cup of filling in center of each chicken breast. Fold edges of chicken over stuffing, then roll to form a bundle. Tie each bundle with a 20-inch piece of cotton twine. Rub surface of bundles with remaining garlic mixture.

Combine bread crumbs, flour, remaining 1 teaspoon salt, and 1/8 teaspoon pepper in a shallow bowl. Roll bundles in seasoned crumbs until well coated. Set aside.

In a pressure cooker, heat remaining 1/4 cup olive oil until hot. Carefully place bundles in oil, brown on one side, and turn. Place broccoli over chicken. Pour broth over broccoli. Secure lid. Over high heat, develop steam to high pressure. Reduce heat to maintain pressure and cook 8 minutes. Release pressure according to manufacturer's directions. Remove lid.

Use tongs to remove broccoli and arrange around edge of a platter. Place chicken bundles in center; snip and remove strings. Spoon juices over broccoli and chicken. Serve with steamed rice. Makes 6 servings.

Broccoli Filling
Finely chop broccoli and mix with oil, green onion, lemon juice, and cheese.

Cook's Note: Meat mallets are a flat-based utensil with a handle. They can be easily found at fine houseware shops. Use two sheets of waxed or parchment paper and sandwich the chicken between the sheets before pounding flat.

Steamed Chicken

Steamed chicken can be enjoyed as is or used in other dishes calling for cooked chicken.

8 chicken pieces
1/2 teaspoon salt

1/4 teaspoon pepper
1 cup water

Season chicken pieces with salt and pepper.
  Pour water into pressure cooker. Insert steam rack. Place chicken pieces on top of rack. Secure lid. Over high heat, develop steam to high pressure. Reduce heat to maintain pressure and cook 10 minutes. Release pressure according to manufacturer's directions. Remove lid.
  Using tongs, place steamed chicken on a platter. Makes 6 servings.

Chicken in Light Mustard Cream

Choose your favorite prepared mustard to accent this chicken dish.

1/4 cup prepared mustard
1 1/2 teaspoons salt
1/4 teaspoon pepper
1 (2 1/2- to 3-lb.) frying chicken, cut into 8
   pieces (2 inches thick)
1/3 cup seasoned bread crumbs
1/4 cup olive oil

3 shallots, minced
1 garlic clove, crushed
1 cup chicken broth or stock
1 tablespoon sherry
1 teaspoon tomato paste
1/3 cup half-and-half
1 tablespoon potato starch or flour

Blend mustard, salt, and pepper in a small bowl until smooth. Brush on chicken pieces and roll pieces in bread crumbs.

In a pressure cooker, heat oil. Add chicken and sauté in hot oil until brown on all sides, using long-handled tongs to turn. Drain on paper towels. Add shallots and garlic and sauté in oil 1 minute. Stir in broth, sherry, and tomato paste. Blend in remaining seasoned mustard. Add chicken pieces. Secure lid. Over high heat, develop steam to medium-high pressure. Reduce heat to maintain pressure and cook 9 minutes. Release pressure according to manufacturer's directions. Remove lid.

Place chicken on a platter. Combine half-and-half and potato starch in a small bowl. Stir into cooking liquid and cook, stirring, over medium heat until thickened. Spoon sauce over chicken. Makes 6 servings.

Cook's Note: For a deep mustard flavor, consider trying a dark mustard. The general rule to remember in selecting the perfect mustard is that light-colored mustards give a more delicate flavor. The darker the mustard, the more intense the mustard flavor.

Chicken Paprika

This Hungarian stew is a personal favorite. The spices have been chosen to balance the flavors perfectly.

1/4 cup olive oil
1 large onion, diced
2 garlic cloves, crushed
1 carrot, finely diced
1/3 cup chopped parsley
3 pounds chicken, cut into 8 pieces (2 inches thick)
2 cups canned or fresh chicken broth or stock
1 tablespoon sherry
2 tablespoons tomato paste
1 teaspoon salt

1/4 teaspoon pepper
2 tablespoons paprika
1 teaspoon dried thyme
1 teaspoon caraway seeds, crushed and in a cheesecloth bag
1 bay leaf
1/2 cup sour cream
2 tablespoons butter, softened
1 1/2 tablespoons potato starch or flour
Cooked noodles or spaetzle (page 130) to serve

In a pressure cooker, heat oil. Add onion, garlic, carrot, and parsley and sauté in hot oil 3 minutes. Add chicken pieces, stir well, and cook 1 minute. Stir in broth, sherry, tomato paste, salt, pepper, paprika, thyme, caraway seeds, and bay leaf. Secure lid. Over high heat, develop steam to high pressure. Reduce heat to maintain pressure and cook 10 minutes. Release pressure according to manufacturer's directions. Remove lid.

Remove bay leaf and caraway bag. Cook chicken mixture over medium-high heat 1 minute.

Combine sour cream, butter, and potato starch. Blend into chicken mixture and cook, stirring, until mixture begins to thicken.

Serve immediately over hot noodles or spaetzle. Makes 6 servings.

Cook's Note: Remember to first crush the caraway seeds in a mortar and pestle, then tie in a bag. If you skip the bag, count on having lots of seeds in the stew.

Chicken Piccata

Italian in origin, this is full of lemon flavor. Always use fresh-squeezed lemon juice for the best results.

6 chicken breast halves
1/2 cup all-purpose flour
1/4 cup olive oil
4 shallots, minced
3 garlic cloves, crushed
3/4 cup chicken broth
1/3 cup fresh lemon juice
1 tablespoon sherry

2 teaspoons salt
1/4 teaspoon white pepper
1 teaspoon dried basil
1 cup pimento-stuffed green olives, minced
1/4 cup sour cream
1 tablespoon potato starch or flour
1/4 cup (1 ounce) grated Fontinella cheese
1 lemon, thinly sliced, to garnish

Lightly dust chicken pieces with flour. In pressure cooker, heat oil. Add chicken breasts, two at a time, and sauté in hot oil until brown on all sides, using long-handled tongs to turn. Set aside.

Add shallots and garlic and sauté in oil, scraping bottom of pan to loosen browned particles remaining from chicken. Stir in broth, lemon juice, sherry, salt, pepper, basil, and olives. Mix well. Add chicken, placing pieces skin side down. Secure lid. Over medium-high heat, develop steam to high pressure. Reduce heat to maintain pressure and cook 10 minutes. Release pressure according to manufacturer's directions. Remove lid.

Stir chicken mixture, then transfer chicken to serving platter, and cover to retain heat.

Whisk sour cream and starch together. Stir into cooking liquid and cook over medium heat 1 minute, stirring constantly.

Spoon sauce over chicken. Sprinkle with cheese and garnish with lemon slices. Makes 6 servings.

Cook's Note: To easily dust the chicken pieces with flour, place flour and chicken in a bag. Shake up and down several times, coating the chicken. Remove chicken pieces and shake off excess flour.

Chicken with Arborio Rice & Peppers

The bacon in this robust Italian stew adds a traditional flavor.
The red and green bell pepper strips give the dish flavor and eye appeal.

1/4 cup olive oil

3 pounds chicken, cut into serving pieces (2 inches thick)

3 slices bacon, cut into 1-inch pieces

2 large onions, coarsely chopped

4 garlic cloves, crushed

1/2 cup chopped parsley

1 1/2 cups arborio rice

1 teaspoon dried rosemary, crushed between palms

1 1/2 teaspoons dried basil, crushed between palms

2 bay leaves

4 cups chicken broth

1 cup tomato puree

1 tablespoon brown sugar

1 1/2 teaspoons salt

1/2 teaspoon black pepper

1 red bell pepper, cut lengthwise into 1/8-inch strips

1 green bell pepper, cut lengthwise into 1/8-inch strips

1/2 cup (2 ounces) grated Fontinella or Parmesan cheese, divided

In a pressure cooker, heat oil. Add chicken and sauté in hot oil until brown on all sides, using long-handled tongs to turn. Do not crowd chicken while browning. Transfer chicken to paper towels and reserve. Add bacon, onions, garlic, and parsley and sauté in oil 3 minutes, scraping bottom of pan to loosen any particles remaining from browned chicken. Add rice, rosemary, basil, and bay leaves. Stir well and cook 1 minute. Add broth, tomato puree, brown sugar, salt, and black pepper. Stir in chicken pieces. Secure lid. Over high heat, develop steam to high pressure. Reduce heat to maintain pressure and cook 9 minutes. Release pressure according to manufacturer's directions. Remove lid.

Stir chicken and rice mixture. Add bell peppers. Secure lid. Over high heat, develop steam to medium pressure. Insert a heat diffuser between pan and heat, and cook 2 minutes.

Release pressure according to manufacturer's directions. Remove lid.

Discard bay leaves. Stir half of cheese into chicken and rice mixture. Transfer to a serving platter and sprinkle with remaining cheese. Makes 6 servings.

Chicken Pot Pie with Puff Pastry

This pot pie is done in two steps. First, the luscious filling is cooked in the pressure cooker, then it is baked to perfection.

1/4 cup olive oil
1 large onion, sliced
2 garlic cloves, crushed
3 carrots, cut into 1/2-inch slices
1 cup (1/2-inch slices) celery
6 chicken breast halves, skin removed, boned, and cut into 1 1/2- to 2-inch pieces
1 1/2 cups chicken broth or stock
1 tablespoon fresh lemon juice
2 teaspoons sherry
1/2 pound mushrooms, stems and caps thinly sliced
3 medium-size potatoes, peeled and diced

1 1/2 teaspoons salt
1/4 teaspoon freshly ground white pepper
1 teaspoon dried tarragon
1/2 teaspoon dried thyme
1/2 teaspoon ground fennel
1 bay leaf
1 1/2 cups frozen green peas
1/2 cup half-and-half or milk
2 tablespoons butter, softened
2 tablespoons potato starch or flour
1 (17 1/4-oz.) package frozen puff pastry, thawed

In pressure cooker, heat oil. Add onion, garlic, carrots, and celery and sauté in hot oil over medium-high heat 2 minutes. Add chicken pieces, stir, and cook 1 minute. Stir in broth, lemon juice, sherry, mushrooms, potatoes, salt, pepper, and herbs. Secure lid. Over high heat, develop steam to high pressure. Reduce heat to maintain pressure and cook 6 minutes. Release pressure according to manufacturer's directions. Remove lid.

Stir in peas. Bring to a boil and cook 1 minute. Reduce heat to medium. Discard bay leaf.

Combine half-and-half, butter, and potato starch in a small bowl, blending until smooth. Stir into chicken mixture until thoroughly mixed. Pour into a 13" x 9" baking dish or 6 individual ovenproof dishes.

Preheat oven to 400°F (205°C). On a lightly floured surface, roll puff pastry, overlapping pastry sheets, into a rectangle slightly larger than baking dish, or cut out rounds slightly larger than individual dishes. Brush away excess flour. Place pastry over chicken mixture. Using a paring knife, trim away excess dough around dish edges. Place dish on a baking sheet.

Bake 12 minutes or until golden brown. Makes 6 servings.

Cook's Note: Frozen puff pastry is available in the frozen food section at most major grocery stores.

Chicken with Two Peppers & Noodles

This tasty pasta dish is wonderful with any available noodle. The flavor is in the robust sauce!

1/4 cup olive oil
1 large white onion, sliced
3 garlic cloves, crushed
4 chicken breast halves, each cut into halves
   (2 inches thick)
1 red bell pepper, sliced lengthwise
1 green bell pepper, sliced lengthwise
3 cups chicken broth or stock
1 (8-oz.) can tomato sauce
1 tablespoon fresh lemon juice
2 tablespoons brown sugar

2 teaspoons salt
1/4 teaspoon freshly ground black pepper
2 teaspoons dried basil
1 1/2 teaspoons dried oregano
1/2 teaspoon ground fennel
1 bay leaf
1 (16-oz.) bag dried noodles
1/2 cup (2 ounces) grated Fontinella cheese
1/2 cup (2 ounces) grated Parmesan cheese

In a pressure cooker, heat oil. Add onion and sauté in hot oil 3 minutes. Add garlic, chicken pieces, and peppers. Sauté over medium-high heat 3 minutes, stirring occasionally. Stir in broth, tomato sauce, lemon juice, brown sugar, salt, black pepper, and herbs. Add noodles and stir again. Secure lid. Over high heat, develop steam to high pressure. Insert a heat diffuser between pan and heat. Reduce heat to maintain pressure and cook 10 minutes. Release pressure according to manufacturer's directions. Remove lid.

Combine cheeses. Discard bay leaf. Stir chicken and noodle mixture and transfer to a serving bowl. Sprinkle with cheese. Makes 6 servings.

Parisian Chicken Stew

The delicate asparagus and pea pods are added to this tasty stew just before the last two minutes of cooking. The pressure cooking process is interrupted to add the veggies. If they were added at the beginning, the vegetables would be overcooked and unrecognizable.

1/3 cup olive oil
1 large carrot, thinly sliced
4 leeks (white part only), sliced
3 garlic cloves, crushed
1 (3-lb.) chicken, cut into 8 pieces (1 1/2 to 2 inches thick)
1/2 cup chicken broth
1/4 cup white wine
2 tablespoons fresh lemon juice
3 carrots, cut into 2-inch pieces
3 medium-size potatoes, peeled and quartered
2 teaspoons salt
1/2 teaspoon white pepper

1/3 cup chopped parsley
1 1/2 tablespoons dried tarragon
1 teaspoon fresh rosemary or 1/2 teaspoon dried rosemary
2 medium-size tomatoes, quartered, seeds removed
3 tablespoons chopped fresh chives or 1 1/2 tablespoons dried chives
1 pound asparagus, trimmed and cut into 2-inch pieces
1 pound snow peas, ends removed
1/3 cup sour cream
3 tablespoons all-purpose flour

In a pressure cooker, heat oil. Add thinly sliced carrot, leeks, and garlic and sauté in hot oil over medium-high heat 2 minutes. Add chicken pieces and cook 2 minutes, turning chicken once or twice. Stir in broth, wine, lemon juice, carrot pieces, potatoes, salt, pepper, parsley, tarragon, and rosemary. Secure lid. Over high heat, develop steam to medium-high pressure. Reduce heat to maintain pressure and cook 8 minutes. Release pressure according to manufacturer's directions. Remove lid.

Stir chicken mixture. Add tomatoes, chives, asparagus, and peas. Stir gently. Secure lid. Over high heat, develop steam to medium-high pressure. Reduce heat to maintain pressure and cook 2 minutes. Release pressure according to manufacturer's directions. Remove lid.

Stir chicken and vegetable mixture gently. Combine sour cream and flour in a small bowl; add by spoonfuls to stew and cook, stirring, until slightly thickened and creamy. Taste and correct seasoning if needed. Makes 6 servings.

Cook's Note: Individual servings of stew may be frozen up to 2 months. Thaw in refrigerator.

Greek Chicken & Rice Pilaf

This is a Greek peasant dish. The oregano and dried fennel are traditional flavors.

1/3 cup olive oil
1 large onion, diced
2 garlic cloves, crushed
1 (2 1/2- to 3-lb.) chicken, cut into 8 pieces
4 cups chicken broth or stock
2 cups long-grain white rice
1 tablespoon brown sugar

1/4 cup tomato paste
2 teaspoons salt
1/2 teaspoon white pepper
1 teaspoon dried oregano
1/2 teaspoon ground fennel
2 bay leaves

In pressure cooker, heat oil. Add onion and garlic and sauté in hot oil over medium-high heat 2 minutes. Add chicken pieces and cook 2 minutes, stirring occasionally. Stir in broth, rice, brown sugar, tomato paste, salt, pepper, oregano, fennel, and bay leaves. Secure lid. Over high heat, develop steam to high pressure. Insert a heat diffuser between pan and heat. Reduce heat to maintain pressure and cook 9 minutes. Release pressure according to manufacturer's directions. Remove lid.

Shake chicken and rice mixture well and stir to distribute cooking liquid. Discard bay leaves. Makes 6 servings.

Middle Eastern Chicken with Yogurt

Spearmint, not to be mistaken for peppermint, is the symbol of hospitality in homes in the Middle East. Plentiful in the summer, spearmint may be dried or frozen for future use. Greek mythology claims the nymph Mentha angered Pluto's wife, who turned Mentha into an aromatic herb.

6 chicken breast halves
1/3 cup all-purpose flour
1/4 cup olive oil
6 green onions, minced
3 garlic cloves, crushed
1/3 cup minced parsley
1 tablespoon dried spearmint
1 teaspoon ground cumin

1/2 cup chicken broth
3 tablespoons fresh lemon juice
1 (8-oz.) container yogurt
1 teaspoon salt
1/2 teaspoon freshly ground white pepper
2 egg yolks
1 tablespoon potato starch or flour
Steamed rice and vegetables to serve

Dust chicken pieces with flour, shaking to remove excess flour. In a pressure cooker, heat oil. Add chicken and sauté in hot oil until browned, turning. Transfer chicken to a platter and reserve. Add green onions, garlic, and parsley and sauté in hot oil 2 minutes. Add chicken and stir. Sprinkle with spearmint and cumin. Add broth, lemon juice, yogurt, salt, and pepper. Stir well. Secure lid. Over high heat, develop steam to high pressure. Reduce heat to maintain pressure and cook 10 minutes. Release pressure according to manufacturer's directions. Remove lid.

Place chicken in a serving dish. Ladle out 1/2 cup of hot broth and whisk into egg yolks. Add potato starch to yolk mixture. Stir into cooking liquid. Cook, stirring, until thickened.

Serve with steamed rice and vegetables. Makes 6 servings.

Paella

This saffron-flavored Spanish stew is full of fresh ingredients including shellfish, chicken, herbs, spices, and vegetables.

1/4 pound bacon, cut into 1-inch pieces
2 large onions, sliced
1/4 cup olive oil
4 garlic cloves, crushed
1 3/4 cups long-grain white rice
6 chicken pieces (legs, thighs, breasts, wings)
5 cups chicken broth or stock
1/4 cup plus 2 tablespoons tomato paste
1/2 cup bottled clam juice
3 tablespoons fresh lemon juice
2 tablespoons sherry
1 tablespoon brown sugar
1/4 cup chopped parsley

2 1/2 teaspoons salt
1 pinch saffron threads
1/2 teaspoon paprika
3/4 teaspoon crushed red pepper flakes
2 teaspoons dried oregano
2 bay leaves
1/2 cup sliced green bell pepper
1/2 pound sea scallops
1/2 pound shrimp in shell
1 cup green peas
1 cup pitted ripe olives
6 lemon slices to garnish

In a pressure cooker, sauté bacon until crisp. Add onions and oil and cook over medium-high heat 2 minutes. Add garlic, rice, and chicken pieces. Cook, stirring frequently, 1 minute. Add broth, tomato paste, clam juice, lemon juice, sherry, brown sugar, parsley, salt, saffron, paprika, pepper flakes, oregano, and bay leaves. Stir well. Secure lid. Over high heat, develop steam to high pressure. Insert a heat diffuser between pan and heat. Reduce heat to maintain pressure and cook 8 minutes. Release pressure according to manufacturer's directions. Remove lid.

Add bell pepper, scallops, and shrimp to chicken mixture. Stir well. Secure lid. Cook over medium-low heat 3 minutes, shaking pan occasionally. Release pressure according to manufacturer's directions. Stir mixture, add peas and olives, and stir again. Discard bay leaves. Taste and correct seasoning if needed.

Spoon into a serving dish. Garnish with lemon slices. Makes 6 servings.

Cook's Note: Saffron is an orange-yellow stamen from the crocus flower and it is known as the world's most expensive spice. It takes about 12,000 to 14,000 stigmas to prepare an ounce of dried saffron.

Stewed Chicken with Orzo & Vegetables

Because frozen green peas need very little cooking, they are added to this zesty dish at the very end of the cooking time, adding color and flavor.

1/4 cup olive oil
6 chicken breast halves, each cut into halves
2 onions, minced
3 garlic cloves, crushed
3 carrots, sliced
1/2 cup chopped parsley
1 1/2 cups orzo
4 cups chicken broth or stock

1/3 cup tomato sauce
1 1/4 teaspoons salt
1/4 teaspoon red pepper flakes
2 teaspoons dried basil
1 teaspoon dried oregano
1 cup frozen green peas
1/4 cup (1 ounce) grated Fontinella or Parmesan cheese

In a pressure cooker, heat oil. Add chicken and sauté in hot oil, lightly browning on both sides. Set aside and reserve. Add onions, garlic, carrots, and parsley and sauté in hot oil 2 minutes, stirring frequently and scraping bottom of cooker. Stir in orzo and cook 1 minute. Add broth, tomato sauce, salt, pepper flakes, basil, and oregano. Stir well. Place chicken over orzo mixture. Secure lid. Over high heat, develop steam to high pressure. Insert a heat diffuser between pan and heat. Reduce heat to maintain pressure and cook 10 minutes. Release pressure according to manufacturer's directions. Remove lid.

Add peas to chicken and orzo mixture, stir well, and cook over medium heat 2 minutes, stirring frequently.

Transfer chicken and rice to a platter and sprinkle with cheese. Makes 6 servings.

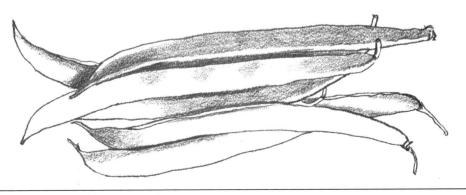

Tortellini & Chicken in Parmesan Cream Sauce

Tortellini is available both dried and fresh in most supermarkets.
These tender bundles are deliciously wonderful.

3 slices bacon, cut into 1/2-inch pieces
1/4 cup butter
4 shallots, minced
3 tablespoons minced parsley
4 chicken breast halves, skin removed, boned
1 small carrot, thinly sliced
1 (8-oz.) package dried, cheese-filled tortellini
1 teaspoon dried tarragon
2 cups chicken broth

1 pound asparagus, trimmed and cut into
  2-inch pieces
1/2 cup half-and-half or milk
3 tablespoons butter, softened
1/3 cup grated Parmesan cheese plus extra
  to serve
2 teaspoons potato starch or flour
Parsley sprigs to garnish

In a pressure cooker, sauté bacon 2 minutes. Add butter, shallots, and parsley. Stir well and sauté 2 minutes. Stir in chicken, carrot, tortellini, and tarragon. Add broth and mix well. Secure lid. Over high heat, develop steam to high pressure. Insert a heat diffuser between pan and heat. Reduce heat to maintain pressure and cook 6 minutes. Release pressure according to manufacturer's directions. Remove lid.

Stir in asparagus. Remove diffuser. Secure lid. Over high heat, develop steam to medium-high pressure. Insert heat diffuser between pan and heat. Reduce heat to maintain pressure and cook 2 minutes. Release pressure according to manufacturer's directions. Remove lid.

Combine half-and-half, butter, 1/3 cup cheese, and potato starch in a small bowl. Blend thoroughly. Gradually add to chicken and tortellini mixture, gently stirring over medium heat until sauce begins to thicken and becomes creamy.

Transfer chicken and tortellini with sauce to serving platter. Sprinkle with additional cheese and garnish with parsley sprigs. Makes 6 servings.

Fish & Shellfish

Fish has very little fat or muscle and therefore will cook very quickly. Cook on low pressure 2 minutes per 1 inch of thickness. Always reduce the steam quickly under cold water at the end of the cooking cycle. Select pieces of fish that are uniform in thickness for best results. For steaming, wrap the fish in cheesecloth or parchment paper. If a golden appearance is desired, sauté the fish in very hot oil before sealing the pressure cooker and cooking the fish.

Fish is an excellent alternative to red meat. If you're "fishing" for a change of taste, check my chart (page 106). Select seafood with a flavor and texture close to your usual catch. Try the substitutes in your favorite recipes. Plan on 8 ounces boned fish per serving.

Store fish in ice water or on ice until ready to use. Avoid fish that has a strong odor or hazy eyes. The flesh should be firm.

FISH BUYER'S GUIDE

Mild Flavor
Cod
Crab
Grouper
Lake perch
Lobster
Monkfish
Ocean catfish
Pollock
Rockfish
Scrod
Sheepshead
Skate
Trout
Walleye pike
Whitefish

Moderate Flavor
Buffalo
Butterfish
Flounder
Halibut
Mahimahi
Mullet
Ocean perch
Orange roughy
Pompano
Red snapper
Sea bass
Shad
Shark
Smelt
Sole
Sturgeon
Whiting

Full Flavor
Bluefish
Catfish
Haddock
Mackerel
Marlin
Salmon
Smoked fish
Swordfish
Tuna

Lobster Thermidor with Vegetables

This dish is thought to have been named by Napoleon. Traditionally the dish is spooned back into the lobster shells and sprinkled with cheese.

6 lobster tails
2 tablespoons butter
2 tablespoons olive oil
3 shallots, minced
1 garlic clove, crushed
1 tablespoon sherry
1 cup bottled clam juice
1 tablespoon fresh lemon juice
1 tomato, seeds removed and diced

1 teaspoon salt
1/4 teaspoon white pepper
4 carrots, cut into julienne
1 pound mushrooms, sliced
1 cup frozen green peas
1/2 cup half-and-half or milk
1 1/2 tablespoons potato starch or flour
1/2 cup grated Parmesan cheese

Using scissors, cut through center of underside of each lobster tail. Pull meat away from the shells and cut into 1 1/2-inch pieces. Set lobster and shell aside.

In a pressure cooker, heat butter and oil. Add shallots and garlic and sauté 1 minute. Add sherry and stir well. Add clam juice, lemon juice, tomato, salt, and pepper. Mix thoroughly. Add lobster and shells. Secure lid. Over high heat, develop steam to medium pressure. Reduce heat to maintain pressure and cook 3 minutes. Release pressure according to manufacturer's directions. Remove lid.

Add carrots and mushrooms to lobster mixture. Secure lid. Over high heat, develop steam to medium pressure. Reduce heat to maintain pressure and cook 1 minute. Release pressure as quickly as possible according to manufacturer's directions, usually by running unit under cold water. Remove lid.

Remove shells. Stir peas into lobster mixture. Combine half-and-half and potato starch, then stir into lobster mixture and cook over medium heat 1 minute, slowly stirring to blend.

Preheat broiler. Ladle lobster mixture into a heatproof serving dish and sprinkle with Parmesan cheese. Brown under broiler. Makes 6 servings.

Variation

Shrimp, crab, and/or scallops can be substituted for the lobster.

Bouillabaisse

Bouillabaisse is traditionally served in deep soup bowls and topped with a dollop of a garlic-based sauce called Rouille. The sauce gives the soup a pungent flavor and helps thicken the liquid when blended in.

1/4 cup olive oil
3 or 4 leeks (white part only), sliced
1 garlic clove, crushed
1/3 cup chopped parsley
1 carrot, thinly sliced
1 cup tomato sauce
1 cup Rich Fish Stock (page 23)
1 teaspoon grated lemon zest
1 tablespoon sherry
2 teaspoons salt
1/8 teaspoon crushed red pepper flakes
3/4 teaspoon dried thyme
1/2 teaspoon ground fennel
1 large pinch saffron
2 bay leaves
2 tomatoes, quartered and seeds removed

1/2 green bell pepper, sliced
2 celery stalks, cut into 1-inch pieces
1 lobster tail, cut into thirds
1 pound shrimp, shelled and deveined
1 pound flounder, cut into 2-inch pieces
1 pound scallops, rinsed well
Crusty bread to serve

Rouille:
4 garlic cloves, peeled
3 slices bread, crumbled
1/3 cup olive oil
1/4 cup Rich Fish Stock (page 23)
3 drops hot pepper sauce
1/4 teaspoon salt
1 teaspoon dried basil

In a pressure cooker, heat oil. Add leeks, garlic, parsley, and carrot and sauté in hot oil 3 minutes. Stir in tomato sauce, stock, lemon zest, sherry, salt, pepper flakes, thyme, fennel, saffron, and bay leaves. Stir well. Add tomatoes, bell pepper, celery, and lobster. Mix thoroughly. Secure lid. Over high heat, develop steam to medium-high pressure. Reduce heat to maintain pressure and cook 3 minutes. Release pressure as quickly as possible according to manufacturer's directions, usually under cold, running water. Remove lid.

Gently stir lobster and vegetable mixture. Add shrimp, flounder, and scallops. Secure lid. Over high heat, develop steam to high pressure. Reduce heat to maintain pressure and cook 2 minutes. Release pressure as quickly as possible according to manufacturer's directions, usually under cold, running water. Remove lid.

Pour Bouillabaisse into serving bowls and add a dollop of Rouille. Serve with hunks of crusty bread. Makes 6 servings.

Rouille

Combine garlic, bread, oil, stock, hot pepper sauce, salt, and basil in a food processor or blender. Process until smooth.

Cook's Note: When seafood is purchased for Bouillabaisse, reserve all trimmings for fish stock. The trimmings may be frozen for later use.

Louisiana Seafood Creole

This Creole stew is rich in flavor and contains all the flavors we associate with Louisiana cuisine. There is just a hint of a spicy aftertaste.

1/3 cup olive oil
3 slices bacon, cut into 1/2-inch pieces
2 large onions, sliced
3 garlic cloves, crushed
1 cup (1/2-inch slices) celery
2 carrots, cut into 1/4-inch slices
1/3 cup chopped parsley
1 cup bottled clam juice
2 tablespoons lemon juice
2 tablespoons sherry
1 cup canned crushed tomatoes
1/4 cup jalapeño salsa
1 tablespoon brown sugar
1 1/2 teaspoons salt
1/2 teaspoon crushed red pepper flakes

1/2 teaspoon red (cayenne) pepper
2 teaspoons paprika
1 teaspoon dried thyme
2 bay leaves
1 pound mushrooms, stems trimmed and caps thinly sliced
1 large green bell pepper, thinly sliced lengthwise
1 cup pimento-stuffed green olives
1 pound bay scallops
1 pound shrimp, peeled and deveined
3 tablespoons butter, softened
2 teaspoons potato starch or flour
Pressure Steamed Rice (page 146) to serve

In a pressure cooker, heat oil. Add bacon, onions, and garlic and sauté in hot oil 2 minutes. Add celery, carrots, and parsley. Cook 1 minute. Stir in clam juice, lemon juice, sherry, tomatoes, salsa, brown sugar, salt, pepper flakes, cayenne, paprika, thyme, and bay leaves. Stir well. Secure lid. Over high heat, develop steam to high pressure. Reduce heat to maintain pressure and cook 2 minutes. Release pressure according to manufacturer's directions. Remove lid.

Stir mushrooms, bell pepper, olives, scallops, and shrimp into tomato mixture. Stir well. Secure lid. Over high heat, develop steam to medium pressure. Reduce heat to maintain pressure and cook 2 minutes. Release pressure as quickly as possible according to manufacturer's directions, usually under cold, running water. Remove lid.

Gently stir seafood mixture. Discard bay leaves. Combine butter and potato starch, blending to paste consistency. Add 1 tablespoon at a time to seafood mixture, stirring to blend, and cook over medium heat 1 minute. Serve over steamed rice. Makes 6 servings.

French Fish Stew

Serve this stew from the French seashore with slices of crusty French bread.

2 pounds orange roughy, haddock, or cod
(1 1/2-inch-thick pieces)
6 shallots, thinly sliced
2 garlic cloves, crushed
1/3 cup olive oil
1 green bell pepper, sliced
1 carrot, sliced
3 medium-size red potatoes, thinly sliced
1/2 cup bottled clam juice

1 (14 1/2-oz.) can whole tomatoes,
undrained, mashed
1 tablespoon fresh lemon juice
1/4 cup chopped parsley
1 teaspoon salt
1/8 teaspoon freshly ground white pepper
2 tablespoons bouquet garni in cheesecloth
bag (see Cook's Note, below)
1 cup pitted ripe olives
2 tablespoons butter, softened
2 tablespoons all-purpose flour

Cut fish into 3-inch pieces.

In a pressure cooker heat oil. Add shallots and garlic and sauté in hot oil. Add bell pepper, carrot, and potatoes. Stir well. Add clam juice, tomatoes, lemon juice, parsley, salt, pepper, and bouquet garni. Mix thoroughly. Place fish over vegetables. Secure lid. Over high heat, develop steam to medium-high pressure. Reduce heat to maintain pressure and cook 3 minutes. Release pressure as quickly as possible according to manufacturer's directions, usually under cold, running water. Remove lid.

Carefully transfer fish and vegetables to a platter. Stir in olives. Combine butter and flour, blending to paste consistency. Stir paste into cooking liquid and cook, stirring, 1 minute or until thickened. Spoon sauce over fish and vegetables. Makes 6 servings.

Variation

If orange roughy is not available, any firm-fleshed fish like cod, haddock, or swordfish will substitute well.

Cook's Note: Bouquet garni is available already bagged or you may mix your own by crushing together 1 crumbled bay leaf, 2 teaspoons dried parsley, 1 teaspoon dried thyme, and 1 teaspoon dried marjoram and tying in a cheesecloth bag or placing in a tea infuser. If you would prefer to use fresh herbs, use the recipe on page 191.

Lobster Fricassee

The fricassee is lovely and delicate in flavor.

3 (1/2- to 3/4-lb.) lobster tails
1/4 cup butter
4 shallots, minced
1 garlic clove, crushed
1 carrot, diced
1/2 pound mushrooms, cut into 1/4-inch slices
1/4 cup cognac or brandy
1 cup bottled clam juice
2 teaspoons fresh lemon juice
1 parsley sprig

3/4 teaspoon salt
1/4 teaspoon white pepper
1 teaspoon dried tarragon
1 bay leaf
3 tablespoons butter, softened
1/3 cup half-and-half
1 tablespoon potato starch or flour
6 puff pastry shells or hard rolls, cut into halves
   and centers removed

Using scissors, cut along bottom of each lobster tail, pulling meat away from the shell. Cut the meat lengthwise in halves, then cut each half into 2-inch pieces. Set meat and large shell pieces aside.

In a pressure cooker, melt butter. Add shallots, garlic, and carrot and sauté 2 minutes. Stir in mushrooms. Add cognac and cook 1 minute, stirring frequently. Add clam juice, lemon juice, parsley, salt, pepper, tarragon, and bay leaf. Stir well. Add lobster and large shells, stirring gently to mix with vegetables and liquid. Secure lid. Over high heat, develop steam to medium pressure. Reduce heat to maintain pressure and cook 3 minutes. Release pressure as quickly as possible according to manufacturer's directions, usually under cold, running water. Remove lid.

Using long-handled tongs, remove large shells and bay leaf. Stir well.

Combine butter, half-and-half, and potato starch, blending well. Stir into cooking liquid and cook, stirring, over medium heat until mixture thickens. Serve over puff pastry shells or hard rolls. Makes 6 servings.

Cook's Note: Puff pastry shells are available in the frozen food section of your grocery store.

Red Snapper with Potatoes, Green Pepper, & Tomatoes

Red snapper is a delicious ocean fish found off the U.S. coast. This one-dish Italian meal is flavor-filled, with seasonings blended for ultimate satisfaction.

1/4 cup olive oil
1 large onion, sliced
2 garlic cloves, crushed
1 green bell pepper, sliced
6 ripe tomatoes, cut into sixths and seeds
  removed
4 potatoes, cut into 1/2-inch slices
1 cup bottled clam juice

1 tablespoon fresh lemon juice
1 1/2 teaspoons salt
1/4 teaspoon crushed red pepper flakes
1 1/2 teaspoons dried basil
1 teaspoon dried oregano
6 (6-oz.) red snapper fillets (1 inch thick)
1 1/2 tablespoons potato starch or flour
1/4 cup grated Parmesan cheese

In a pressure cooker, heat oil. Add onion and garlic and sauté in hot oil 2 minutes. Add bell pepper and tomatoes. Stir well and cook 1 minute. Add potatoes, clam juice, lemon juice, salt, pepper flakes, and herbs. Stir well. Secure lid. Over high heat, develop steam to medium-high pressure. Reduce heat to maintain pressure and cook 4 minutes. Release pressure according to manufacturer's directions. Remove lid.

Gently stir vegetable mixture. Place red snapper over vegetables. Secure lid. Over medium-high heat, develop steam to medium. Reduce heat to maintain pressure and cook 2 1/2 minutes. Release pressure quickly according to manufacturer's directions, usually under cold, running water. Remove lid.

Using slotted spatula, carefully transfer red snapper and potatoes to a platter. Cover to retain heat.

Blend potato starch into 1/4 cup of the sauce, stir into remaining sauce, and cook, stirring, 1 minute or until sauce thickens. Spoon sauce over red snapper and potatoes. Sprinkle with cheese. Makes 6 servings.

Salmon Steak with Leeks in Yogurt Dill Sauce

Salmon is commonly known as a saltwater fish; however, it has become landlocked in freshwater lakes during the spawning season. In general, the lake salmon is less flavorful than the sea salmon. This fresh-flavored dish will be a low-fat favorite.

2 tablespoons olive oil
4 leeks (white part only), cut into 1/4-inch
   slices
2 garlic cloves, crushed
2 tablespoons minced parsley
1 cup bottled clam juice
2 tablespoons fresh lemon juice
1 teaspoon sherry

1 1/2 teaspoons salt
1/4 teaspoon white pepper
2 teaspoons dried dill weed or 1/3 cup
   chopped fresh dill
6 salmon steaks (1 inch thick)
1 teaspoon prepared horseradish
1/4 cup low-fat yogurt
2 teaspoons potato starch or flour

In a pressure cooker, heat oil. Add leeks, garlic, and parsley and sauté in hot oil 2 minutes. Add clam juice, lemon juice, sherry, salt, pepper, and dill. Stir well. Place salmon steaks in cooking liquid. Secure lid. Over high heat, develop steam to medium-high pressure. Reduce heat to maintain pressure and cook 3 minutes. Release pressure quickly according to manufacturer's directions, usually under cold, running water. Remove lid.

   Transfer salmon steaks to a serving platter. Cover to retain heat. Combine horseradish, yogurt, and potato starch in a small bowl. Whisk into cooking liquid and cook over medium heat, stirring, 1 minute or until mixture thickens. Spoon sauce over salmon. Makes 6 servings.

Salmon Steak with Spinach & Lemon Herb Sauce

Salmon flesh varies from white to bright red. If you can find the white, it is usually firmer. The salmon on a bed of fresh spinach topped with a lemon sauce makes a deliciously refreshing combination.

1 cup water
2 1/2 teaspoons salt, divided
2 (10-oz.) packages fresh spinach, well rinsed
    and leaves cut into halves
2 tablespoons olive oil
1 medium-size onion, finely diced
2 garlic cloves, crushed
2 tablespoons minced parsley

1 cup bottled clam juice
1/4 cup fresh lemon juice
1/4 teaspoon white pepper
1 1/2 teaspoons dried thyme
6 salmon steaks (1 inch thick)
2 egg yolks
1 teaspoon potato starch or flour

Pour water into a pressure cooker. Stir in 1 teaspoon salt. Place spinach in cooker, pushing away from edge. Secure lid. Over high heat, develop steam to medium-high pressure. Reduce heat to maintain pressure and cook 3 minutes. Release pressure according to manufacturer's directions. Remove lid.

Stir spinach thoroughly. Drain through a colander, place on a platter, cover, and keep warm in a warm oven.

Wipe moisture from pressure cooker. Heat oil in pressure cooker. Add onion, garlic, and parsley and sauté in hot oil 2 minutes. Stir in clam juice, lemon juice, remaining 1 1/2 teaspoons salt, pepper, and thyme. Place salmon steaks in cooking liquid. Secure lid. Over high heat, develop steam to medium-high pressure. Reduce heat to maintain pressure and cook 3 minutes. Release pressure quickly according to manufacturer's directions, usually under cold, running water. Remove lid.

Using a slotted spatula, transfer salmon to a platter. Cover to retain heat. Stir egg yolks and potato starch into 1/3 cup of the cooking liquid and pour back into pan. Cook, stirring, over medium heat until mixture begins to thicken. Remove from heat.

To serve, arrange a portion of spinach on 6 plates. Top each with a salmon steak and spoon sauce over salmon. Makes 6 servings.

Salmon & Vegetables with Fennel Sauce

This easy, one-dish meal is elegant enough for company.

1/4 cup olive oil
4 leeks (white part only), sliced
1 garlic clove, crushed
1 cup bottled clam juice
1 tablespoon fresh lemon juice
2 tablespoons sherry
1 (8-oz.) can tomato sauce
1 1/2 teaspoons salt
1/4 teaspoon pepper

1 1/2 teaspoons crushed dried fennel
4 carrots, cut into 1-inch pieces
1 cup (1-inch pieces) celery
1/2 cup minced parsley
3 potatoes, cut into 1/2-inch slices
6 (6-oz.) salmon fillets (1 1/2 inches thick)
3 tablespoons butter, softened
1 teaspoon potato starch or flour

In a pressure cooker, heat oil. Add leeks and garlic and sauté in hot oil 2 minutes. Add clam juice, lemon juice, sherry, tomato sauce, salt, pepper, and fennel. Stir well. Stir in carrots, celery, parsley, and potatoes. Secure lid. Over high heat, develop steam to high pressure. Reduce heat to maintain pressure and cook 4 minutes. Release pressure according to manufacturer's directions. Remove lid.

Place salmon fillets over vegetables. Secure lid. Over medium-high heat, develop steam to medium-low pressure. Reduce heat to maintain pressure and cook 3 minutes. Release pressure according to manufacturer's directions. Remove lid.

Using a slotted spatula, transfer salmon and most of vegetables to a serving platter. Cover to retain heat.

Drain remaining vegetables through a strainer, place vegetables on platter, and return cooking liquid to pressure cooker. Cook over medium-high heat. Stir in butter and potato starch to paste consistency and cook until slightly thickened. Spoon sauce over salmon and vegetables. Makes 6 servings.

Seafood in Crust

You'll want to lick the plate because the flavor combination of the seafood and the garlic bread container is so good. Serve with steamed fresh green peas.

6 hard-crust rolls
1/2 cup butter, melted, plus 5 tablespoons butter, divided
3 garlic cloves, crushed, divided
1/4 cup olive oil
6 shallots, sliced
1/4 cup chopped parsley
2 carrots, sliced
1 cup bottled clam juice
2 tablespoons fresh lemon juice
1 tablespoon sherry

1 1/2 teaspoons salt
1/4 teaspoon white pepper
2 tablespoons bouquet garni in cheesecloth bag (see page 191)
1 pound shrimp, shelled and deveined, or scallops
1 1/2 pounds scrod or whitefish, boned and cut into 2-inch pieces
1 pound mushrooms, sliced
2 tablespoons butter, softened
1/4 cup half-and-half
1 tablespoon potato starch or flour

Using a bread knife, slice tops from rolls. Remove soft bread from inside rolls, leaving a shell. Blend melted butter and 2 garlic cloves in a small bowl. Brush inside of rolls with garlic butter. Set aside.

In a pressure cooker, heat oil and 3 tablespoons butter. Add shallots, remaining garlic, parsley, and carrots and sauté 2 minutes. Stir in clam juice, lemon juice, sherry, salt, pepper, and bouquet garni. Mix thoroughly. Fold in seafood and mushrooms. Secure lid. Over high heat, develop steam to medium pressure. Reduce heat to maintain pressure and cook 3 minutes. Release pressure quickly according to manufacturer's directions, usually under cold running water. Remove lid.

Combine 2 tablespoons softened butter, half-and-half, and potato starch in a small bowl. Gradually stir into seafood mixture. Cook, stirring, over medium heat 2 minutes or until mixture thickens. Ladle seafood mixture with sauce into rolls, allowing it to overflow onto serving dish. Makes 6 servings.

Cook's Note: The bread from the center of the rolls may be processed in a food processor into crumbs for another use.

Sea Scallops with Fresh Vegetables

Two species of scallops are found in our fish markets. The large and meaty sea scallop and the much smaller and sweeter bay scallop found on the East Coast of the United States. Try them both and form your own opinion as to your favorite. Made with either one, this one-dish scallop casserole is luscious and colorful.

1/4 cup olive oil
5 shallots, sliced
1 garlic clove, crushed
1 carrot, thinly sliced
1/4 cup chopped parsley
1/4 cup Rich Fish Stock (page 23) or clam juice
2 tablespoons fresh lemon juice
2 1/2 pounds sea scallops or bay scallops
1 pound asparagus, trimmed and cut into 2-inch pieces

1 pound mushrooms, sliced
3/4 pound cherry tomatoes
1/2 pound snow peas, ends removed
1 teaspoon salt
1/8 teaspoon white pepper
1 teaspoon dried basil
1/4 teaspoon grated ginger root
1 1/2 tablespoons butter, softened
1 1/2 tablespoons all-purpose flour

In a pressure cooker, heat oil. Add shallots, garlic, carrot, and parsley and sauté in hot oil 2 minutes. Stir in stock, lemon juice, scallops, asparagus, mushrooms, tomatoes, peas, salt, pepper, basil, and ginger root. Gently stir. Secure lid. Over high heat, develop steam to medium pressure. Reduce heat to maintain pressure and cook 2 minutes. Release pressure quickly according to manufacturer's directions, usually under cold, running water. Remove lid.

   Combine butter and flour in a small bowl, blending to paste consistency. Stir into scallop mixture and cook, stirring, over low heat 1 minute. Makes 6 servings.

Whitefish Fillets with Vegetables in Parchment

The whitefish is popular because of its lovely, sweet flavor.

1/4 cup plus 2 tablespoons butter, softened
1/4 cup fresh lemon juice
3 shallots or green onions (white part only), minced
2 garlic cloves, crushed
1/4 cup minced parsley
1 teaspoon salt
1/4 teaspoon white pepper

1 teaspoon dried thyme
3 pounds whitefish, cut into 6 pieces
2 medium-size potatoes, peeled and cut into 1/8-inch sticks
3 carrots, cut into 3-inch sticks
1 zucchini, cut into 1/2-inch slices
1 1/2 cups water
Green salad to serve

Combine butter, lemon juice, shallots, garlic, parsley, salt, pepper, and thyme in a small bowl. Whisk until well mixed.

Cut 6 (8-inch) pieces of parchment paper. Butter one side of each piece. Lay a fillet on each piece of parchment. Rub or brush lemon butter mixture over fillets. Place several pieces of potato on each fillet, then carrots, then zucchini. Wrap parchment, envelope style, around each fillet to enclose. Place in steam basket, crisscross to fit. Pour the water into pressure cooker. Insert steam basket.

Secure lid. Over high heat, develop steam to high pressure. Reduce heat to maintain pressure and cook 5 minutes. Release pressure according to manufacturer's directions. Remove lid.

Remove steam basket. Using spatula, transfer bundles to a serving dish. Unwrap fish and vegetables and serve with salad. Makes 6 servings.

Cook's Note: Before preparing whitefish, rinse the fish thoroughly and look around the bottom area for a band of fat, usually grayish pearl in color. With a sharp knife, trim away this band or it will add a fishy flavor to the dish.

Stuffed Flounder or Sole Rolls with Sauce & Asparagus

A member of the flatfish family, the flounder is a light textured, delicately flavored fish.
Combined with delicate spring asparagus, it makes a lovely one-dish presentation.

Scallop Stuffing (see opposite)
2 tablespoons fresh lemon juice
1 1/2 teaspoons salt, divided
1/8 teaspoon white pepper
6 sole or flounder fillets (1 inch thick), rinsed
1 cup bottled clam juice
1/2 teaspoon dried thyme
1 1/2 pounds asparagus, trimmed
2 egg yolks
1/4 cup half-and-half or milk
1/4 cup butter, softened

Scallop Stuffing:
2 tablespoons butter
3 tablespoons olive oil
2 green onions, minced
2 tablespoons minced parsley
1/2 teaspoon dried thyme
1/3 pound bay scallops
4 slices bread, crumbled
1/4 cup bottled clam juice or water
1 tablespoon fresh lemon juice
1/4 teaspoon salt
Dash of pepper

Prepare stuffing.

Combine lemon juice, 1 teaspoon salt, and pepper in a small bowl. Rub mixture over both sides of fillets. Place fillets on work surface, skin side up. Spoon 2 tablespoons of stuffing on widest end of each fillet and roll up.

Pour clam juice into pressure cooker. Add thyme, 1/2 teaspoon salt, and remaining lemon juice mixture. Stir well. Place each fish roll in steam basket. Top with asparagus. Insert basket in cooker. Secure lid. Over high heat, develop steam to high pressure. Reduce heat to maintain pressure and cook 3 minutes. Release pressure according to manufacturer's directions. Remove lid.

Remove basket from cooker. Transfer fish and asparagus to a serving platter. Cover to retain heat.

Combine egg yolks, half-and-half, and butter in a small bowl. Whisk mixture into cooking liquid over medium-high heat. Cook, stirring, until thickened. Do not boil. Spoon sauce over fish rolls and asparagus. Makes 6 servings.

Scallop Stuffing

Heat butter and oil in a large skillet. Add green onions and parsley and sauté 2 minutes. Add thyme and scallops, stir well, and cook over high heat 2 minutes. Stir in bread crumbs, clam juice, lemon juice, salt, and pepper.

Place mixture in a food processor or blender. Process until a thick paste consistency. Set aside.

Smoked Salmon with Fettuccine in Cream Sauce

This versatile pasta dish makes a great entrée, side dish, or first course.
The pasta cooks in a thyme-flavored broth.

1/4 cup olive oil
2 cups fettuccine
4 cups chicken broth
3/4 teaspoon salt
1/4 teaspoon white pepper
1 teaspoon dried thyme
3 tablespoons butter, cut into small pieces

1/2 cup sour cream or yogurt
1 pound smoked salmon, trout, or whitefish,
    separated into bite-size pieces
2 green onions, chopped
1/3 cup freshly grated Parmesan or Fontinella
    cheese

In a pressure cooker, heat oil. Add fettuccine, broth, salt, pepper, and thyme. Secure lid. Over high heat, develop steam to high pressure. Reduce heat to maintain pressure and cook 8 minutes. Release pressure according to manufacturer's directions. Remove lid.

Drain fettuccine through a colander and place in a pasta bowl. Toss with butter and sour cream. Add fish and green onions, tossing gently until mixed. Sprinkle with cheese. Makes 6 servings.

Whitefish with Pureed Vegetable Sauce

The fresh pureed vegetable sauce will appeal to the most discriminating palate.

1/4 cup fresh lemon juice, divided
1 1/4 teaspoons salt, divided
1/4 teaspoon white pepper, divided
2 pounds whitefish fillets (1/2 inch thick),
   cut into 6 pieces
2 tablespoons butter
1/4 cup olive oil

1 leek (white part only), sliced
1 cup bottled clam juice
2 tablespoons fresh lemon juice
1 1/2 cups frozen green peas
1/2 teaspoon dried thyme
1/4 cup sour cream
Steamed potatoes or rice to serve

Combine 2 tablespoons lemon juice, 1/2 teaspoon salt, and 1/8 teaspoon pepper in a small bowl. Rub mixture over all sides of fillets. Dot with butter. Set aside.

In a pressure cooker, heat oil. Add leek and sauté in hot oil 2 minutes. Stir in clam juice, lemon juice, peas, 3/4 teaspoon salt, 1/8 teaspoon pepper, and thyme. Stir well. Layer fillets in steam basket, separating each layer with parchment paper. Place basket in pressure cooker. Secure lid. Over high heat, develop steam to medium-high pressure. Reduce heat to maintain pressure and cook 3 minutes. Release pressure according to manufacturer's directions. Remove lid.

Remove steam basket and transfer fish to a serving platter. Cover to retain heat.

Pour cooking liquid and peas into a food processor or blender. Add sour cream. Blend until smooth. Spoon sauce over fish. Serve with steamed potatoes or rice. Makes 6 servings.

Variation

If you prefer to use a less fatty fish in this recipe, you may substitute any fish of your choice, but the fish should be the same thickness or the cooking time adjusted.

Steamed Whole Fish with Lemon Parsley Sauce

If you prefer the fish to remain straight during the pressure cooking process, insert a wooden skewer through the entire fish, beginning at the head and ending at the tail. Otherwise, the fish will curve, which I think makes a lovely presentation.

1 (12- to 14-inch) whole pickerel, trout, or
  whitefish with head and tail, ready to cook
2 tablespoons fresh lemon juice
1 teaspoon salt
1/4 teaspoon white pepper
1 1/2 cups water
Parsley to garnish
1 pimento-stuffed green olive

Lemon Parsley Sauce:
1/2 cup butter, melted
1 garlic clove, crushed
1/3 cup minced parsley
3 egg yolks
1/3 cup fresh lemon juice
1/2 teaspoon salt
1/8 teaspoon white pepper
1/2 cup chopped, pitted olives

Rinse fish. Combine lemon juice, salt, and white pepper in a small bowl. Brush surface and cavity of fish with mixture. Measure thickness of fish.

Place fish, cavity side down, in steam basket, curving fish along side of basket or placing across basket. Pour water into pressure cooker and insert steam basket. Secure lid. Over high heat, develop steam to medium-high pressure. Reduce heat to maintain pressure and cook 2 1/2 minutes per inch of fish. If you have a fish 3 inches thick, it will take about 7 1/2 minutes (multiplying the thickest part by 2 1/2 minutes). Release pressure according to manufacturer's directions. Remove lid.

Remove steam basket. Carefully transfer fish to a serving platter. Fish will remain curved. Peel skin from fish. Prepare sauce. Keep fish warm. Garnish gills with parsley. Cut a pimento-stuffed olive in half and insert each half into eye cavities. Garnish platter with dill or parsley sprigs. Serve with sauce. Makes 6 servings.

Lemon Parsley Sauce

Melt butter in a saucepan. Add garlic and parsley and sauté until softened. Gradually whisk in egg yolks, lemon juice, salt, and pepper. Cook, stirring, over low heat until thickened. Stir in olives.

Vegetables &
Side Dishes

Vegetables cooked in the pressure cooker are absolutely wonderful. The color remains vibrant, the nutrients are retained, and best of all, the flavors are more pronounced than in conventional cooking. Vegetables cook quickly and it is important to follow the timing chart precisely.

For successful pressure cooked vegetables: keep the vegetables uniform in size and use accurate minimum water amounts as recommended by the manufacturer. Timing begins after the pressure is reached. Reduce the steam quickly at the end of the cooking cycle, usually by releasing the pressure under cold, running water.

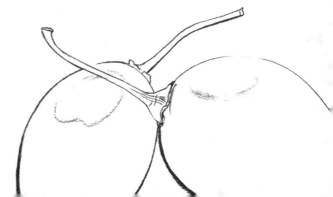

Selecting Fine Vegetables

When shopping, look for firm stems and leaves. If the vegetables appear wilted, do not buy them as they have already lost nutrients. Refrain from purchasing vegetables with blemishes or large, dark holes or spots.

VEGETABLE COOKING TIMES

Vegetable	Cut	Minutes	Whole (min)	Frozen (min)	Pressure
Acorn squash	halves	12			high
Artichoke	quartered	3	10	3	medium-high
Asparagus			2	3	medium-low
Beans, green		3			medium
Beets	1/2" slices	3	14	5	high
Broccoli	flowerets	3		3	medium-high
Broccoli	spears	2			medium-high
Brussels sprouts			4	5	medium-high
Cabbage	shredded	2			medium-high
Cabbage	quartered	6			medium-high
Carrots	1/2" slices	3		4	high
Cauliflower	flowerets	2		3	medium-high
Cauliflower	quartered	4			medium-high
Celery	1" slices	2			medium-high
Corn	ears	2		5	high

Vegetable	Cut	Minutes	Whole (min)	Frozen (min)	Pressure
Eggplant	1" slices	2			medium
Endive			8		high
Escarole			8		high
Fennel root	1/2" slices	2	5		medium-high
Okra	pods	3		4	medium-high
Onion	1" slices	2			medium-high
Parsnips	quartered	4	10		high
Peas	pods	2		4	medium-low
Potatoes	2" cuts	7	10		high
Potatoes (new)	1 1/2"–2"		8		high
Rutabagas	2" cuts	7		8	high
Spinach			3	4	medium-high
Sweet potato	2" cuts	6	12		high
Tomatoes	quartered	2	5		medium-high
Turnips	1/2" slices	2	10		high
Zucchini	1" slices	2			medium-high

Layers of vegetables may be steamed or pressure cooked together with very little mingling of flavors. Add the minimum amount of water required, according to the manufacturer's directions for your cooker. Insert the steam basket. Layer vegetables, separating with parchment paper or stacking in ovenproof containers.

Remember to release the steam quickly after timing is reached. Run cold water over lid to quickly reduce the pressure.

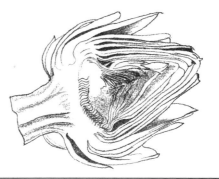

BEAN & LENTIL COOKING TIMES

Type of Beans	Minutes	Pressure
Black-eyed peas	10	high
Garbanzo beans	20	high
Kidney beans	12	high
Lima beans	10	high
Michigan beans	12	high
Navy beans	15	high
Peas	10	high
Pinto beans	12	high
Turtle beans (black beans)	15	high
Lentils	10	high

Conventional Soaking

Soak dried peas and beans overnight. Measure beans, place in a bowl, add water in twice the amount of the measured beans and 1 teaspoon salt. Let stand overnight or at least 6 hours. Drain, then cook as directed.

Pressure Cooker Soaking (Quick Soaking)

Pour 4 cups water, 1 teaspoon salt and 1 cup dried peas or beans into pressure cooker. Secure lid. Over high heat, develop steam to high pressure. Reduce heat to maintain pressure and cook 2 minutes. Quickly reduce pressure by running cold water over cooker. Remove lid. Drain peas or beans, then cook as directed.

Because beans are starchy and the starches can scorch, always use a heat diffuser on the range burner after pressure is reached.

Allow 3 cups liquid for each 1 cup of soaked beans (see opposite). Add 1 tablespoon oil to the cooking water. This prevents excessive starchy foam. Allow steam to slowly reduce at the end of the cooking cycle; beans need the extra steam time and improve in texture.

RICE COOKING TIMES

Type of Rice	Minutes	Pressure
Basmati rice	7	medium-high
Converted rice	7	medium-high
Long-grain rice	7	medium-high
Long-grain brown rice	15	high
Wild rice	25	high
Arborio rice	15	high

Rice is fluffy and perfect when prepared in the pressure cooker. Always use the heat diffuser on the burner after pressure is reached, or starches from rice will settle on the bottom and scorch.

Allow 2 1/4 cups water or broth for each 1 cup of rice, along with 1 teaspoon salt and 1 tablespoon oil. Allow steam to reduce slowly at the end of the cooking cycle. Grains like the extra moisture and improve in texture.

PASTA COOKING TIMES

Type of Pasta	Minutes	Pressure
Cavatelli	18	high
Egg noodles	7	medium-high
Elbow macaroni	7	medium-high
Macaroni	8	high
Spaghetti	8	high
Spaghetti (thin)	7	high
Spinach noodles	6	medium-high
Fresh noodles	5	medium-high
Tortellini	5	medium-high
Ravioli	4	medium-high

Pasta is wonderful when prepared in the pressure cooker.

Be sure ingredients do not exceed half the capacity of the cooker. Always add 2 tablespoons oil to the cooking liquid to minimize the starchy foam that develops during cooking. Allow steam to reduce slowly at the end of the cooking cycle. Use heat diffuser on the burner after pressure is reached.

Autumn Ratatouille

About 1/4 cup Ratatouille folded into an omelet makes an out-of-this-world dish!

1/4 cup olive oil
2 large onions, sliced
3 garlic cloves, crushed
1/3 cup chopped parsley
2 carrots, cut into 3/4-inch slices
1 large eggplant, peeled and cut into 2-inch cubes
1 1/2 pounds zucchini, cut into 2-inch pieces
1 (15-oz.) can whole, peeled tomatoes, crushed
1 green bell pepper, sliced lengthwise
2 large potatoes, cut into 1/4-inch slices

1/2 cup beef, chicken, or vegetable stock
1 tablespoon light brown sugar
1 teaspoon salt
3/4 teaspoon crushed red pepper flakes
1 teaspoon dried leaf oregano
1/4 teaspoon fennel powder
2 tablespoons bouquet garni (see page 191) in cheesecloth bag
2 bay leaves
3 tablespoons butter, softened
3 tablespoons all-purpose flour

In a pressure cooker, heat oil. Add onions, garlic, parsley, and carrots and sauté in hot oil 2 minutes. Add eggplant, zucchini, tomatoes, bell pepper, potatoes, stock, brown sugar, salt, pepper flakes, oregano, fennel, bouquet garni, and bay leaves. Stir well. Secure lid. Over high heat, develop steam to high pressure. Reduce heat to maintain pressure and cook 6 minutes. Release pressure quickly according to manufacturer's directions. Remove lid.

Gently stir vegetables. Discard bay leaves.

Combine butter and flour in a small bowl, making a paste; gradually add to vegetables, and cook, stirring, until slightly thickened. Makes 6 to 8 servings.

Variation

If you want to eliminate the butter in the flour paste, add 1/3 cup seasoned dried bread crumbs and stir a few seconds. This will thicken the ratatouille's extra juices

Beets

*Ruby red fresh beets are available year round in vegetable markets and produce departments.
However, their flavor is best from May to November. Select beets with greens attached.
Look for firm bulbs without blemishes.*

2 cups water
6 (3-inch) whole beets, unpeeled, whole or
   quartered, greens removed

1/2 teaspoon salt

Pour water into a pressure cooker. Add beets and salt. Secure lid. Over high heat, develop steam to high pressure. Reduce heat to maintain pressure and cook whole beets 14 minutes or quartered beets 8 minutes. Release pressure according to manufacturer's directions. Remove lid.
  Drain beets in a colander, then rinse under cold, running water, rubbing to remove skins. The skins should release easily. Makes 6 servings.

Broccoli with Lemon Butter

*Broccoli is available year round in the U.S., but the price may vary depending on the season.
Look for a deep green color. Stalks should not be dry.*

1/2 cup water
1 bunch broccoli, stems peeled and trimmed,
   split into serving pieces
3 tablespoons butter, melted

1 tablespoon fresh lemon juice
1/4 teaspoon salt
1/4 cup grated Asiago cheese (optional)

Pour water into a pressure cooker. Layer broccoli in steam basket and place in cooker. Secure lid. Over high heat, develop steam to high pressure. Reduce heat to maintain pressure and cook 3 minutes. While broccoli cooks, whisk butter, lemon juice, and salt together in a small bowl. Set aside.
  Quickly release steam according to manufacturer's directions. Remove lid.
  Remove steam basket and carefully transfer broccoli to a serving dish. Spoon lemon sauce over broccoli and sprinkle with cheese, if using. Makes 6 servings.

Brown Rice with Fresh Vegetables

This easy dish using both rice and vegetables is prepared in one-half the time that brown rice usually takes.

1/4 cup olive oil
1/2 medium-size onion, diced
2 large garlic cloves, crushed
1/4 cup minced parsley
1 large carrot, cut into bite-size pieces
1 1/2 cups long-grain brown rice
1 teaspoon salt

1/4 teaspoon white pepper
1 teaspoon dried leaf thyme
1 bay leaf
3 1/2 cups chicken broth or stock
2 tablespoons fresh lemon juice
1/2 pound broccoli, stems peeled and
　　trimmed, cut into bite-size pieces

In a pressure cooker, heat oil. Add onion, garlic, parsley, and carrot and sauté in hot oil 3 minutes. Add rice, salt, pepper, thyme, and bay leaf. Stir and cook 1 minute. Add broth and lemon juice. Secure lid. Over high heat, develop steam to high pressure. Insert a heat diffuser between pan and heat. Reduce heat to maintain pressure and cook 15 minutes. Release pressure according to manufacturer's directions. Remove lid.

Add broccoli to rice mixture. Secure lid. Over high heat, develop steam to high pressure. Insert a heat diffuser between pan and heat. Reduce heat to maintain pressure and cook 1 minute. Quickly release steam according to manufacturer's directions. Remove lid.

Discard bay leaf. Using 2 large forks, toss broccoli and rice mixture and spoon into a serving dish. Makes 6 to 8 servings.

Cook's Note: Stirring rice into oil will retard the foamy starch in the cooker during cooking.

Cauliflower & Broccoli Parmesan

What could be easier and more appetizing than this healthy side dish of deep green and contrasting white flowerets?

2 tablespoons olive oil
1 cup water or chicken broth or stock
2 tablespoons fresh lemon juice
2 tablespoons chopped parsley
1/2 teaspoon salt

1/8 teaspoon pepper
1/2 teaspoon dried oregano
1/2 head cauliflower, cut into flowerets
1/2 bunch broccoli, stems peeled and
   trimmed, cut into flowerets
1/4 cup grated Parmesan cheese

In a pressure cooker, combine oil, broth, lemon juice, parsley, salt, pepper, and oregano. Stir well. Layer cauliflower and broccoli in steam basket and place in cooker. Secure lid. Over high heat, develop steam to high pressure. Reduce heat to maintain pressure and cook 3 minutes. Quickly release steam according to manufacturer's directions. Remove lid.

Remove steam basket and place vegetables on a platter. Spoon 1/4 of cooking liquid over vegetables and sprinkle with cheese. Makes 6 servings.

Cook's Note: Uncooked cauliflower and broccoli will hold a week in the refrigerator. Unwashed, the vegetables should be stored in a plastic bag with a few sprinkles of water.

Fennel with Grated Parmesan

Fresh fennel is found in recipes from France and Italy. Look for firm white bulbs and crisp, green leaves with no blemishes. Fennel is available in late winter and early spring.

1/4 cup olive oil
1 leek (white part only), sliced
6 fennel bulbs, trimmed and cut into 1/2-inch
   slices
1 cup chicken broth

1 1/2 teaspoons salt
1/4 teaspoon white pepper
1 teaspoon dried basil
1/4 cup grated Parmesan cheese

In a pressure cooker, heat oil. Add leek and sauté 2 minutes in hot oil. Add fennel and gently stir. Add broth, salt, pepper, and basil and stir again. Secure lid. Over high heat, develop steam to medium-high pressure. Reduce heat to maintain pressure and cook 2 minutes.

Quickly release pressure according to manufacturer's directions. Remove lid. Carefully drain fennel and transfer to a serving platter. Sprinkle with cheese. Makes 6 servings.

Carrots & Broccoli with Indian Dressing

Flavor and nutrients reside in the carrot skins. Refrain from peeling unless necessary.

2 cups water
2 pounds broccoli, stems peeled, trimmed, and
   split below flowerets
3 carrots, cut into 3-inch strips
1/2 teaspoon ground fennel
1/2 teaspoon salt
1/4 teaspoon pepper
Indian Dressing (see opposite)

Indian Dressing:
2 tablespoons fresh lemon juice
1/3 cup olive oil
2 garlic cloves, crushed
1/2 teaspoon salt
1/8 teaspoon red (cayenne) pepper
1/8 teaspoon curry powder
1/8 teaspoon prepared mustard

Pour water into a pressure cooker. Insert steam basket. Layer vegetables in basket. Sprinkle seasonings over vegetables. Secure lid. Over high heat, develop steam to medium pressure. Reduce heat to maintain pressure at low and cook 3 minutes. Quickly release steam according to manufacturer's directions. Remove lid.

Remove steam basket.

Prepare dressing. Layer vegetables on a platter and sprinkle with dressing. Makes 6 servings.

Indian Dressing
Combine lemon juice, oil, garlic, salt, cayenne, curry powder, and mustard in a measuring cup with spout. Whisk until thoroughly blended.

Cauliflower with Herbed Pea Sauce

This dish makes a lovely and colorful addition to any meal.
The green pea puree is vibrant against the cauliflower.

1/4 cup olive oil
3 green onions, minced
1 slice bacon, cut into 1/2-inch pieces
1 cup chicken broth or stock
2 cups frozen green peas
2 tablespoons lemon juice
1 teaspoon salt

1/8 teaspoon white pepper
1/2 teaspoon dried basil
1 large head cauliflower, stems trimmed and
   cut into flowerets
1/4 cup sour cream
1/2 cup (2 ounces) shredded Cheddar cheese,
   divided

In a pressure cooker, heat oil. Add green onions and bacon and sauté in hot oil 2 minutes. Stir in broth, peas, lemon juice, salt, pepper, and basil. Layer cauliflower in steam basket. Place basket over pea mixture in cooker. Secure lid. Over high heat, develop steam to medium pressure. Reduce heat to maintain pressure and cook 4 minutes. Quickly release steam according to manufacturer's directions. Remove lid.

Remove steam basket and place cauliflower on a serving platter. Cover to retain heat.

Pour peas and cooking liquid into a food processor or blender. Add sour cream and 1/4 cup cheese. Process until smooth. Spoon sauce over cauliflower and sprinkle with remaining cheese. Makes 6 servings.

Dilled Red Cabbage & Basmati Rice

Basmati rice has a fragrance like that of roasting pecans.

1/4 cup olive oil
2 leeks, thinly sliced
1 garlic clove, crushed
1 cup basmati rice
2 cups chicken broth
2 teaspoons lemon juice

1/3 cup chopped parsley plus extra to garnish
1 teaspoon salt
1/8 teaspoon pepper
2 teaspoons dried dill weed
1/2 head red cabbage, coarsely sliced

In a pressure cooker, heat oil. Add leeks and garlic and sauté in hot oil 2 minutes. Add rice and cook 1 minute. Stir in broth, lemon juice, parsley, salt, pepper, and dill. Secure lid. Over high heat, develop steam to high pressure. Insert a heat diffuser between pan and heat. Reduce heat to maintain pressure and cook 6 minutes. Release pressure according to manufacturer's directions. Remove lid. Remove diffuser.

Add cabbage to rice mixture, using 2 forks to toss until mixed. Secure lid. Over high heat, develop steam to high pressure. Insert heat diffuser between pan and heat. Reduce heat to maintain pressure and cook 3 minutes. Release pressure according to manufacturer's directions. Remove lid.

Using 2 forks, gently toss cabbage and rice mixture and spoon into a serving dish. Sprinkle with chopped parsley. Makes 6 servings.

Cook's Note: The heat diffuser, a curved piece of metal, prevents scorching while rice cooks. During the cooking process, rice starches settle on the bottom of the vessel and the heat diffuser prevents direct contact with heat.

Fettuccine with Parsley Butter

*Pasta can be cooked in the pressure cooker just until tender to the bite
if cooking times are followed correctly.*

2 tablespoons olive oil
1/2 pound fettuccine
3 cups chicken broth or water
1 teaspoon salt
1/4 teaspoon white pepper

1/2 teaspoon dried summer savory, crushed
1/4 cup butter, softened
1/4 cup chopped parsley
1/4 cup grated Fontinella or Parmesan cheese

In a pressure cooker, heat oil. Stir fettucine into hot oil. Add broth, salt, pepper, and savory. Secure lid. Over high heat, develop steam to high pressure. Reduce heat to maintain pressure and cook 8 minutes. Release pressure according to manufacturer's directions. Remove lid.
  Drain fettuccine through a colander and return to cooker. Add butter and parsley, mixing gently until fettuccine is well coated. Pour into a serving bowl. Sprinkle with cheese. Makes 6 servings.

Variation

Short egg noodles may be substituted in this delicate cream dish.

Garbanzo Beans

Dried garbanzo beans, also known as chickpeas, are firmer, nuttier in flavor, and sweeter than the canned ones. They can be added to soups, stews, or salads or make a delicious Hummus (page 11).

1 pound (2 cups) garbanzo beans (chickpeas)
6 cups water
4 cups water or chicken broth

1 teaspoon salt
1/8 teaspoon white pepper

Place beans in a bowl with 6 cups water. Let stand 4 hours. Drain.

In pressure cooker, combine soaked beans, 4 cups water or broth, and seasonings. Stir well. Secure lid. Over high heat, develop steam to high pressure. Reduce heat to maintain pressure and cook 20 minutes. Release pressure according to manufacturer's directions. Remove lid.

Stir beans and let stand 2 minutes. Drain through a colander. Makes 4 cups.

Cook's Note: Garbanzo beans may be frozen up to 3 months. Thaw in refrigerator.

Glazed Carrots with Pecan, Apricot, & Raisin Sauce

Carrots may be used in many vegetable medleys and seasoned with herbs and spices from every cuisine in the world. Serve this dish with roasted turkey, chicken, or pork.

1 cup orange juice
1 pound carrots, cut julienne into 3-inch strips
1/4 cup apricot preserves
1/2 cup golden raisins

1 teaspoon brown sugar
1/8 teaspoon nutmeg
1 tablespoon cornstarch
1/3 cup toasted pecans, chopped (see Cook's Note, page 158)

Pour orange juice into a pressure cooker. Stir in carrots, preserves, raisins, brown sugar, and nutmeg. Secure lid. Over medium-high heat, develop steam to medium pressure. Reduce heat to maintain low pressure and cook 3 minutes. Quickly release pressure according to manufacturer's directions. Remove lid.

Gently stir carrots. Sprinkle cornstarch into 1/2 cup of cooking liquid and stir to mix thoroughly. Cook over medium heat 1 minute. Stir in pecans. Makes 6 to 8 servings.

Greek Rice & Spinach

This delicate vegetarian dish is enjoyed during Lent in Greece. The fresh flavors blend into a lovely main course or side dish.

1/4 cup olive oil
1 medium-size onion, diced
2 garlic cloves, crushed
1/3 cup minced fresh dill
1/4 cup minced parsley
1 cup long-grain white rice
2 cups water

2 1/2 tablespoons tomato paste
2 tablespoons fresh lemon juice
1 teaspoon salt
1/4 teaspoon pepper
1 (10-oz.) package fresh spinach, stems removed
Lemon wedges to serve

In a pressure cooker, heat oil. Add onion, garlic, dill, and parsley and sauté in hot oil over medium-high heat 1 minute. Add rice, stir, and cook 1 minute. Stir in water, tomato paste, lemon juice, salt, and pepper. Place spinach over rice mixture. Secure lid. Over high heat, develop steam to high pressure. Reduce heat to maintain pressure. Insert a heat diffuser between pan and heat. Cook 8 minutes.

Release pressure according to manufacturer's directions. Remove lid.

Stir rice and spinach until well mixed. Serve with lemon wedges. Makes 6 servings.

Green Beans with Basil

Sometimes the simplest recipes are the tastiest, and this dish is a great accompaniment for any main dish.

1/4 cup olive oil
2 garlic cloves, crushed
1 pound green beans, ends removed
1 cup water or chicken stock

3/4 teaspoon salt
1/8 teaspoon pepper
1 teaspoon dried basil
2 tablespoons butter (optional)

In a pressure cooker, heat oil. Add garlic and sauté in hot oil 1 minute. Stir in beans. Add water, salt, pepper, and basil. Stir well. Secure lid. Over high heat, develop steam to medium-high pressure. Reduce range heat to maintain pressure and cook 3 minutes. Quickly release pressure according to manufacturer's directions. Remove lid.

Stir beans, then drain in a colander. Place beans in a serving dish and dot with butter, if using. Makes 6 to 8 servings.

Cook's Note: Available all year round, green beans should be crisp, green, and free of dark spots.

Hawaiian Acorn Squash

Acorn squash is part of the winter squash family. Peak season availability is fall and winter.
Select a squash heavy in weight. The outside should be firm and smooth.

1 cup toasted pecans, chopped (see Cook's Note, page 158)
1 (8 1/4-oz.) can crushed pineapple, drained
1/4 cup butter, softened
1/3 cup firmly packed brown sugar

3 acorn squash, cut into halves, seeds removed, and pierced with fork tines
2 cups water

Combine pecans, pineapple, butter, and brown sugar in a small bowl. Spoon 1/4 cup of mixture into each squash half. Layer squash in steam basket.

Pour water into a pressure cooker. Insert steam basket. Secure lid. Over high heat, develop steam to high pressure. Reduce heat to maintain pressure and cook 15 minutes. Quickly release pressure according to manufacturer's directions. Remove lid.

Remove steam basket and place squash on a platter. Using a fork, loosen cooked pulp and mix with pineapple stuffing. This is good with roasted turkey, pork, or chicken. Makes 6 servings.

Variation

Buttercup or butternut squash may be substituted in this recipe.

Italian Risotto with Vegetables

The texture of this dish is creamy and deliciously satisfying.

2 tablespoons olive oil
1/4 pound pancetta or bacon, cut into 1-inch
   pieces
6 green onions, coarsely chopped
3 garlic cloves, crushed
1 small carrot, thinly sliced
1/4 cup chopped parsley
1 cup arborio rice
2 3/4 cups chicken broth or stock
1/2 cup tomato sauce

1 tablespoon fresh lemon juice
1 tablespoon brown sugar
1 teaspoon salt
1/4 teaspoon white pepper
1 teaspoon dried rosemary
1 bay leaf
1 cup frozen green peas
1/2 cup grated Fontinella or Parmesan cheese

In a pressure cooker, heat oil. Add pancetta, green onions, garlic, carrot, and parsley and sauté in hot oil 3 minutes. Stir in rice and cook 1 minute, stirring. Add broth, tomato sauce, lemon juice, brown sugar, salt, pepper, rosemary, and bay leaf. Stir well. Secure lid. Over high heat, develop steam to high pressure. Insert a heat diffuser between pan and heat. Reduce heat to maintain pressure and cook 13 minutes. Release pressure according to manufacturer's directions. Remove lid.

Using a wooden spoon, stir rice mixture well. Stir in peas. Cook, uncovered, over medium-high heat 1 minute. Ladle rice into a serving bowl and sprinkle with cheese. Makes 6 to 8 servings.

Cook's Note: Arborio rice, also known as *riso* in Italy, is a round, firm rice, and it takes longer to become tender than long-grain rice.

Mandarin Oranges & Sweet Potatoes

The refreshing orange flavors of the sweet juice complement the delicate sweet potatoes.

3/4 cup plus 2 tablespoons orange juice, divided
4 medium-size sweet potatoes, peeled and cut into 1/2-inch slices
3/4 cup firmly packed brown sugar

1/4 cup butter
1 tablespoon cornstarch
1 (11-oz.) can mandarin oranges, drained, divided

Pour 3/4 cup orange juice into a pressure cooker. Place sweet potatoes in juice and sprinkle with brown sugar. Stir well. Secure lid. Over high heat, develop steam to high pressure. Reduce heat to maintain pressure and cook 4 minutes. Quickly release pressure according to manufacturer's directions. Remove lid.

Using a slotted spoon, remove sweet potatoes and arrange on a platter. Dot sweet potatoes with butter.

Combine cornstarch and remaining 2 tablespoons orange juice in a small bowl. Stir into cooking liquid. Cook, stirring, until thickened. Fold in half of oranges. Ladle sauce over sweet potatoes and garnish with remaining oranges. Makes 6 servings.

Cook's Note: Sweet potatoes, a native of South America, are interchangeable with yams. Most sweet potato recipes are sweet; however, these potatoes are delightful when mashed with a dash of nutmeg and a little butter.

Orzo with Pine Nuts & Spearmint

Orzo resembles rice; however, it is a pasta used by the Greeks and Italians in soups, stews, and other main dishes. The texture of the cooked pasta is substantial and satisfying.

1/4 cup olive oil
4 green onions, diced
1/2 cup pine nuts
1 cup orzo
2 1/2 cups chicken broth
2 tablespoons fresh lemon juice

1 teaspoon salt
1/4 teaspoon white pepper
1 teaspoon dried spearmint leaves, crushed
   between palms
1/3 cup chopped parsley

In a pressure cooker over medium-high heat, heat oil. Add green onions and sauté in hot oil 2 minutes. Add pine nuts and orzo. Stir well and cook 3 minutes, stirring occasionally. Stir in broth, lemon juice, salt, pepper, and spearmint. Secure lid.

Over high heat, develop steam to high pressure. Insert a heat diffuser between pan and heat. Reduce heat to maintain pressure and cook 9 minutes. Release pressure according to manufacturer's directions. Remove lid.

Using fork, toss orzo. Add parsley and toss again. Makes 6 servings.

Maple Pecan Sweet Potatoes

Use pure maple syrup for the best flavor.

1 cup water
1 (1-inch) piece lemon peel
1/2 cup firmly packed brown sugar
1/4 teaspoon salt
3 medium-size sweet potatoes, peeled and cut
   into 1/2-inch slices

1/4 cup butter
1 cup coarsely chopped pecans
1/4 cup maple syrup
1 tablespoon cornstarch
Whole pecans to garnish

Pour water into a pressure cooker and add lemon peel, brown sugar, and salt. Stir in sweet potatoes. Secure lid. Over high heat, develop steam to high pressure. Reduce heat to maintain pressure and cook 4 minutes. Release pressure according to manufacturer's directions. Remove lid.

Using a slotted spoon, transfer sweet potatoes to a serving dish.

In a skillet, melt butter, heating until bubbly. Stir in pecans. Add syrup and cornstarch, stirring to blend. Add to liquid in cooker and cook over medium heat until thickened. Ladle over sweet potatoes. Garnish with whole pecans. Makes 6 servings.

Cook's Note: Select firm potatoes with smooth surfaces that are unblemished. It is best to look for evenly shaped potatoes for uniform cooking.

Noodles Alfredo

Serve this marvelous creamy noodle dish as a main dish or side dish.

2 slices bacon, cut into 1-inch pieces
2 tablespoons olive oil
1 leek (white part only), minced
1 garlic clove, crushed
1 carrot, coarsely diced
2 cups egg noodles
1 1/2 cups chicken broth
1 1/2 cups water
8 cherry tomatoes, cut into halves and seeds removed

1 teaspoon salt
1/8 teaspoon white pepper
1/2 teaspoon dried leaf tarragon
1 cup frozen green peas
1/3 cup whipping cream or yogurt
1/3 cup grated Parmesan cheese
3 tablespoons butter
2 tablespoons chopped parsley to garnish

In pressure cooker, sauté bacon until crisp and add olive oil. Add leek, garlic, and carrot and sauté 1 minute. Stir in noodles, broth, water, tomatoes, salt, pepper, and tarragon. Mix thoroughly. Secure lid. Over high heat, develop steam to high pressure. Insert a heat diffuser between pan and heat. Reduce heat to maintain pressure and cook 8 minutes. Release pressure according to manufacturer's directions. Remove lid.

Stir noodle mixture. Drain in a colander and return noodles to cooker. Stir in peas, cream, cheese, and butter. Cook over medium heat 1 minute, stirring. Transfer to a serving platter and garnish with parsley. Makes 6 servings.

Pea Pods with Ginger Butter

This lovely side dish has the exotic taste of ginger root.

1 pound snow peas, ends and strings removed
1/2 cup chicken broth or water
1 teaspoon salt
1/8 teaspoon white pepper

2 tablespoons butter, softened
1 teaspoon sesame oil
1/2 teaspoon finely grated ginger root or 1/8
   teaspoon ground ginger

In a pressure cooker, combine snow peas, broth, salt, and pepper. Secure lid. Over high heat, develop steam to medium-high pressure. Reduce heat to maintain pressure and cook 2 minutes. Quickly release pressure according to manufacturer's directions. Remove lid.

   Drain snow peas in a colander. Spoon into a serving bowl. Combine butter, oil, and ginger root in a small bowl. Add to peas and toss until peas are well coated. Makes 6 servings.

Cook's Note: Remove any strings from peas or they will seem tough to chew. Simply cut the end and tear away slowly.

Pressure Steamed Rice

A basic recipe that can be used as a foil to spicy dishes, or seasoned as described opposite if serving with grilled meats, fish, or chicken.

2 tablespoons olive oil
1 cup long-grain white rice
2 cups beef or chicken broth or water

3/4 teaspoon salt
2 tablespoons butter or olive oil
Dash of freshly ground pepper

In a pressure cooker, heat oil. Stir rice into hot oil. Add broth and salt. Secure lid. Over high heat, develop steam to high pressure. Insert a heat diffuser between pan and heat. Reduce heat to maintain pressure and cook 8 minutes. Release pressure according to manufacturer's directions. Remove lid.

   Add butter and pepper to rice. Toss to mix thoroughly. Serve hot. Makes 6 servings.

Variation

For a seasoned rice with international flair, select one of the following: 1 teaspoon dried dill weed, 1/2 teaspoon dried oregano, 1 teaspoon dried basil, or 1 teaspoon curry powder.

Savory Rice with Buttered Peas

This colorful dish is good with almost any grilled meat or fish, it's a fail-proof way to perfect rice.

3 tablespoons olive oil
2 green onions, minced
1 garlic clove, crushed
1 cup long-grain white rice
2 cups chicken broth or water

1 teaspoon salt
1/4 teaspoon freshly ground white pepper
1/4 teaspoon dried tarragon
3 tablespoons butter
1 cup frozen green peas, defrosted

In a pressure cooker, heat oil. Add green onions and garlic and sauté in hot oil 1 minute. Stir in rice and cook 1 minute. Add chicken broth and seasonings. Secure lid. Over high heat, develop steam to high pressure. Insert a heat diffuser between pan and heat. Reduce heat to maintain pressure and cook 7 minutes. Release pressure according to manufacturer's directions. Remove lid.

Using a fork, add butter a little at a time and toss to blend with rice. Gently toss in peas. Makes 6 servings.

Variation

Experiment by using basmati rice or brown rice in this recipe. Refer to rice chart for timing (page 129).

Zucchini with Herbed Oil

You'll love the fresh flavors of the Greek Islands with the mixture of lemon juice, olive oil, and feta cheese. The Italians of Southern Italy have a similar dish and prepare it with Romano cheese instead of feta. Either way, you'll enjoy the Mediterranean flavors.

4 tablespoons olive oil, divided
1 leek (white part only), thinly sliced
1 cup chicken broth or water
3 zucchini (1 pound), ends trimmed and cut into 1/2-inch slices

1 teaspoon salt
1/4 teaspoon pepper
1 teaspoon dried rosemary
1/4 cup crumbled feta cheese
2 tablespoons fresh lemon juice

In a pressure cooker, heat 2 tablespoons oil. Add leek and sauté in hot oil 2 minutes. Stir in broth, zucchini, salt, pepper, and rosemary. Stir well. Secure lid. Over high heat, develop steam to medium pressure. Reduce heat to maintain pressure and cook 2 minutes. Quickly release pressure according to manufacturer's directions. Remove lid.

Drain zucchini in a colander and place in a serving dish. Sprinkle with cheese. Whisk remaining 2 tablespoons oil and lemon juice together in a small bowl and drizzle over zucchini. Gently toss until thoroughly mixed. Makes 6 servings.

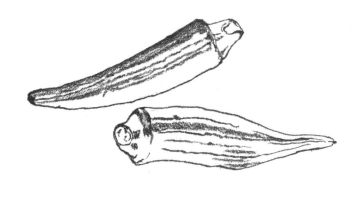

Steamed Escarole with Bacon

For green, leafy vegetables such as fresh spinach, escarole, and endive, plan on eight ounces per person to produce an adequate steamed or boiled serving.

6 slices bacon, cut into 1-inch pieces
4 leeks (white part only), sliced
2 tablespoons olive oil
1 teaspoon salt
2 cups water
3 pounds escarole, stem trimmed
2 tomatoes, seeds removed and cut into
   1-inch pieces
Dressing (see opposite)

Dressing:
1/3 cup olive oil
2 tablespoons fresh lemon juice
1/2 teaspoon salt
1/8 teaspoon white pepper
1/2 teaspoon dried oregano, crushed between
   palms

In a pressure cooker over medium-high heat, sauté bacon until crisp; add leeks and oil. Cook 3 minutes. Stir in salt and water. Add escarole and stir again. Secure lid. Over high heat, develop steam to high pressure. Reduce heat to maintain pressure and cook 8 minutes. While cooking, prepare dressing. Release pressure according to manufacturer's directions. Remove lid.

Stir escarole 1 minute. Drain in a colander, using back of wooden spoon or spatula to press to remove excess liquid from escarole. Place on a serving platter and add tomatoes. Drizzle dressing evenly over vegetables and toss gently until well mixed. Makes 6 servings.

Dressing
Combine oil, lemon juice, salt, pepper, and oregano in a measuring cup with spout. Whisk until thoroughly mixed.

Cook's Notes: Select dark green leaves without dark marks at outer tips. Avoid limp leaves, which have been in the store too long; improper storage causes them to lose nutrients.

Always rinse greens three times in a deep basin of lukewarm water. The warm water relaxes the leaves, releasing the embedded dirt and sand.

Stuffed Peppers & Zucchini

The European flavors of this dish will delight everyone.

3 large green peppers
3 large zucchini
2 1/4 cups beef broth
1/4 cup olive oil
1 large onion, diced
2 garlic cloves, crushed
1/2 cup chopped parsley
1 pound ground lamb, beef, or turkey
1 cup long-grain white rice

1 tablespoon brown sugar
1 tablespoon sherry
1 1/2 teaspoons salt
1/4 teaspoon pepper
2 tablespoons dried dill weed
1 teaspoon dried oregano
1 1/2 cups water
1/3 cup grated Fontinella or Parmesan cheese

Slice tops from bell peppers, remove seeds, rinse well, and set shells aside. Cut zucchini into 4-inch lengths. Using a small spoon, small melon baller, or apple corer, remove pulp from centers of zucchini, leaving 1/4-inch shells. Combine pulp with broth and set aside.

In a pressure cooker, heat oil. Add onion, garlic, and parsley and sauté in hot oil 2 minutes. Crumble meat into onion mixture and stir well. Cook 1 minute. Stir in rice, broth and pulp, brown sugar, sherry, salt, pepper, dill, and oregano. Secure lid. Over high heat, develop steam to high pressure. Insert a heat diffuser between pan and heat. Reduce heat to maintain pressure and cook 8 minutes. Release pressure according to manufacturer's directions. Remove lid.

Stir meat mixture. Spoon 1/6 of mixture into each pepper shell. Cover each with a small piece of foil or parchment paper. Spoon remaining meat mixture into zucchini shells. Cover each end with foil. Pyramid peppers and zucchini in steam basket.

Remove diffuser from burner. Pour water into pressure cooker. Insert steam basket. Secure lid. Over high heat, develop steam to high pressure. Reduce heat to maintain pressure and cook 4 minutes. Quickly release pressure according to manufacturer's directions. Remove lid.

Carefully transfer stuffed vegetables to a serving platter. Remove foil and sprinkle with cheese. Makes 6 servings.

Stuffed Tomatoes

The fresh flavors of this dish are incredibly delicious, especially if made with vine-ripened tomatoes.

6 tomatoes
2 cups beef broth
1 tablespoon brown sugar
1 1/2 teaspoons salt
1/4 teaspoon pepper
1 teaspoon dried oregano
2 teaspoons dried dill weed
1/4 cup olive oil

1 large onion, diced
2 garlic cloves, crushed
1/3 cup chopped parsley
1 pound ground lamb, beef, or turkey
1 cup long-grain white rice
1 1/2 cups seasoned bread crumbs, divided
2 tablespoons butter, softened

Cut 1/2-inch slice from top of each tomato. Using a teaspoon, carefully scoop pulp and juice from each tomato. Place shells in baking pan. In a bowl, mash pulp. Add broth, brown sugar, salt, pepper, oregano, and dill. Stir well and set aside.

In a pressure cooker, heat oil. Add onion and garlic and sauté in hot oil 2 minutes. Add parsley, stir, and cook 1 minute. Crumble meat into onion mixture and cook, stirring to break up meat. Add rice, stir, and cook 1 minute. Add tomato pulp mixture and stir again. Secure lid. Over high heat, develop steam to high pressure. Insert a heat diffuser between pan and heat. Reduce heat to maintain pressure and cook 8 minutes. Quickly release pressure according to manufacturer's directions. Remove lid.

Stir lamb mixture.

Combine bread crumbs and softened butter in a small bowl. Spoon lamb filling into tomato shells, mounding about 1/4 inch above rim. Sprinkle with bread crumb mixture, dividing evenly.

Move broiler shelf to second position nearest heat source. Preheat broiler. Broil stuffed tomatoes 1 minute or until tops are browned. Makes 6 servings.

Variations

Substitute 1/2 teaspoon rosemary and 2 teaspoons dried basil for oregano and dill weed. Use grated Parmesan cheese instead of bread crumbs.

POTATOES

Idaho potatoes are the number-one selling potato in the market and can be used successfully in most potato dishes. Potatoes also come from California, Washington, Michigan, Oregon, and Maine. If available, try the new Yukon gold potato. It has a lovely texture and a hint of butter flavor in its taste.

My preference is the California potato. It has just a little more moisture than the Idaho and the texture is smoother. Use an Idaho or California potato for baked potatoes. For stews and soups, the other varieties work fine. Try a variety of potatoes and form your own preferences.

Potatoes are available in mesh bags or you may select your own. I prefer selecting my own. Look for firm potatoes with smooth skins without bruises or dark spots. Avoid green potatoes.

Potatoes are very nutritious, high in vitamin C, and rich in minerals. Although many believe potatoes are high in calories, potatoes have only about 25 calories per ounce. So enjoy!

Scalloped Potatoes

This popular dish can be made up to a couple of days ahead of time and refrigerated.
Heat in a 325°F (165°C) oven for 20 minutes before serving.

1 cup chicken broth or stock
6 medium-size potatoes, peeled and cut into
   1/4-inch slices
1/2 teaspoon salt
1/8 teaspoon white pepper

1 tablespoon chopped chives
1/3 cup sour cream
1/3 cup milk
2 tablespoons potato starch or flour
Dash of paprika

Pour broth into a pressure cooker. Add potatoes, salt, pepper, and chives. Secure lid. Over high heat, develop steam to high pressure. Reduce heat to maintain pressure and cook 5 minutes. Release pressure according to manufacturer's directions. Remove lid.

  Using a slotted spoon, transfer potatoes to flameproof platter. Preheat broiler. Pour sour cream, milk, and potato starch into cooking liquid in cooker. Cook, whisking to blend, over high heat 1 minute. Pour over potatoes and use 2 forks to gently mix. Sprinkle with paprika and brown under broiler. Makes 6 to 8 servings.

Variation

By adding 1/2 cup shredded Cheddar cheese, the dish is transformed into easy au gratin potatoes. Either way, it's a favorite.

Steamed Whole Potatoes

Toss these with butter and herbs or use in recipes calling for cooked potatoes.

6 (2-inch) potatoes, unpeeled and pricked
   with fork

2 cups water

Place potatoes in steam basket. Pour water into a pressure cooker. Insert steam basket in cooker. Secure lid. Over high heat, develop steam to high pressure. Reduce heat to maintain pressure and cook 10 minutes. Release pressure according to manufacturer's directions. Remove lid.
  Drain potatoes and peel, if desired. Makes 6 servings.

Cook's Note: Potatoes peel very easily after cooking. Pricking the skins allows the moisture to penetrate under the skins.

Parmesan Potatoes with Pesto

*Pesto is traditionally a mixture of fresh basil, freshly grated Parmesan cheese, lemon juice,
oil, and garlic. It's a very aromatic mixture and is wonderful tossed into pasta or rice.
It also gives meat, fish, or poultry an interesting flavor.*

1/4 cup plus 2 tablespoons olive oil, divided
3 leeks (white part only), sliced
3 garlic cloves, crushed, divided
1/3 cup chopped parsley
4 medium-size potatoes, peeled and cut into
   1/2-inch slices
1/2 cup chicken broth or stock

1 teaspoon salt
1/4 teaspoon white pepper
1/4 cup grated Parmesan cheese
1/4 cup minced fresh basil or 1 tablespoon
   dried sweet basil
1 tablespoon fresh lemon juice

In a pressure cooker, heat 1/4 cup oil. Add leeks, 2 garlic cloves, and parsley and sauté in hot oil 3 minutes. Add potatoes and stir well. Add broth, salt, and pepper. Secure lid. Over high heat, develop steam to high pressure. Reduce heat to maintain pressure and cook 5 minutes. Release pressure according to manufacturer's directions. Remove lid.

Drain potatoes in a colander and transfer to a flameproof platter. Preheat broiler. Combine cheese, basil, 1 garlic clove, lemon juice, and 2 tablespoons oil in a small bowl. Add mixture to potatoes, tossing gently until potatoes are evenly coated. Brown under broiler 2 minutes. Makes 6 servings.

Mashed Potatoes

Everyone loves mashed potatoes, especially when they are this easy to prepare.

6 medium-size potatoes, peeled and cut into 1/2-inch slices
1 cup water
1 teaspoon salt

1/2 teaspoon white pepper
3 tablespoons butter
1/4 cup sour cream or milk

In a pressure cooker, combine potatoes, water, salt, and pepper. Secure lid. Over high heat, develop steam to high pressure. Reduce heat to maintain pressure and cook 5 minutes. Release pressure according to manufacturer's directions. Remove lid.

Drain potatoes in a colander and place in a bowl. Using a potato ricer or masher, mash potatoes until a fine-textured consistency. Blend in butter and mash until smooth. Add sour cream and blend thoroughly. Taste and adjust seasoning if needed. Makes 6 to 8 servings.

Variation

To add interest to simple mashed potatoes, add 1 crushed garlic clove, 1/2 teaspoon freshly grated nutmeg, or 1/2 cup chopped green onions. You will find the simple flavor bursts with new excitement.

Desserts

Pressure cooking becomes sweet in this chapter filled with a mouthwatering array of lovely, traditional desserts.

Following these tested recipes, you will realize the heights pressure cooking can reach. Who would imagine creamy cheesecakes, lovely moist bread pudding with a velvety sauce, and lemon curd all cooked to perfection under pressure?

There are several cheesecake recipes that are rich, creamy, and delicious in flavor. The pan size required must fit inside your pressure cooker. Consider using the steamer basket insert that may have come with your unit. Simply line the basket with micro-safe plastic wrap or foil, then proceed with the recipe.

Apple Rum Cinnamon Bread Pudding

Moist with apples and scented with spices, this pudding topped with a dollop of Chantilly Cream is heavenly. The recipe will quickly become a family favorite.

1/2 cup butter, melted, divided
1 cup half-and-half or milk
1 teaspoon rum flavoring
2 large eggs, lightly beaten
1 cup granulated sugar
1/2 cup firmly packed light brown sugar
1 1/2 teaspoons ground cinnamon
1/4 teaspoon grated nutmeg
1 large Granny Smith or McIntosh apple,
    peeled and cut into 1-inch cubes
1/2 cup raisins

3/4 cup chopped toasted walnuts (see Cook's
    Note below)
8 cups (2-inch cubes) Italian or French bread
1 1/2 cups water
Chantilly Cream (optional) (see below)

Chantilly Cream:

2 cups whipping cream
1/3 cup powdered sugar, sifted
1/4 teaspoon vanilla extract
Dash of ground cinnamon

Butter an 8-inch round baking pan or steam basket from pressure cooker (see Appendix) with some of melted butter. If using steam basket, cover outside of basket with foil. Combine remaining butter, half-and-half, rum flavoring, eggs, sugars, cinnamon, and nutmeg in a bowl. Beat until thoroughly blended.

Combine apple, raisins, walnuts, and bread in a large bowl. Pour egg mixture over bread mixture. Toss until bread is well moistened and fruit is thoroughly mixed. Spoon mixture into prepared pan.

Pour water into pressure cooker. Insert steam rack. Prepare foil harness (page 175). Place pan in center of harness and lower into pressure cooker. Fold harness to make a handle over bread pudding. Secure lid. Over high heat, develop steam to high pressure. Reduce heat to maintain pressure and cook 12 minutes. Release pressure according to manufacturer's directions. Remove lid.

Lift pan from pressure cooker and place on a wire rack to cool. Serve hot or cold. Prepare Chantilly Cream, if using, and serve with pudding. Makes 6 to 8 servings.

Chantilly Cream

Whip cream until it begins to thicken. Add powdered sugar, vanilla, and cinnamon. Whip 1 minute or until soft peaks form. Spoon into a serving bowl and refrigerate until ready to serve.

Cook's Note: To toast nuts, preheat oven to 375°F (190°C). Place nuts in a shallow baking pan and bake 7 to 8 minutes or until golden.

Crème Caramel

A classic dish with a hint of lemon prepared in an easy, nontraditional way—
you may never bake this dessert again.

3/4 cup sugar
2 tablespoons water
1/8 teaspoon baking soda
3 large eggs
1 (14-oz.) can sweetened condensed milk

1/2 cup milk or half-and-half
1 teaspoon vanilla extract
1/8 teaspoon grated nutmeg
1/2 teaspoon grated lemon zest
2 cups water

Butter bottom and sides of 6 custard cups or ramekins with 2 tablespoons softened butter. In a small saucepan over medium-low heat, dissolve sugar. It will take 5 to 8 minutes. Add water and cook 1 minute. Gently stir in baking soda and cook a few more minutes until a dark amber. Spoon 2 tablespoons syrup into each cup.

Combine eggs, condensed milk or half-and-half, vanilla, nutmeg, and lemon zest in a bowl. Whisk until well mixed. Pour ½ cup of mixture into each cup. Cover each cup with foil.

Pour water into pressure cooker. Insert steam basket. Place cups, pyramid style, in basket, beginning with three at the bottom. Secure lid. Over high heat, develop steam to medium pressure. Reduce heat to maintain pressure and cook 9 minutes. Release pressure according to manufacturer's directions. Remove lid.

Carefully remove covered cups and place on wire rack. Refrigerate at least 6 hours or overnight. Remove foil. To serve, use a small knife to loosen custard from sides of cups and invert on serving dishes. Makes 6 servings.

Applesauce

You'll never buy applesauce once you've tried this recipe. The cinnamon hearts add a lovely blush and a spicy flavor.

2 pounds McIntosh or Granny Smith apples, peeled, cored, and cut into 1/2-inch slices (about 4 cups)
1 cup canned apple juice
2 tablespoons fresh lemon juice

1/4 cup granulated sugar
1/3 cup firmly packed brown sugar
1/2 teaspoon grated nutmeg
1/4 teaspoon ground cinnamon
1/3 cup red cinnamon candy (optional)

In a pressure cooker, combine apples, apple juice, lemon juice, sugars, nutmeg, cinnamon, and candy, if using. Secure lid. Over high heat, develop steam to medium-high pressure. Reduce heat to maintain pressure and cook 4 minutes. Release pressure according to manufacturer's directions. Remove lid.
  Drain apples through a colander. Place apples in a food processor, blender, or food mill and process until smooth. Serve warm or cold. Store in airtight container in refrigerator up to 3 days. Makes 6 servings.

Spiced Apples

Serve over Belgian waffles, pound cake, French toast, or roll in crêpes for a delicious dessert.

5 Granny Smith apples, peeled, cored, and cut into 1/2-inch slices
1 cup orange juice
3/4 cup granulated sugar
1 cup firmly packed brown sugar

1/4 teaspoon grated nutmeg
1 1/2 teaspoons ground cinnamon
1/2 teaspoon rum flavoring
2 tablespoons cornstarch
1/2 cup water

In a pressure cooker, combine apples, juice, sugars, nutmeg, cinnamon, and rum flavoring. Secure lid. Over high heat, develop steam to high pressure. Reduce heat to maintain pressure and cook 3 minutes. Release pressure according to manufacturer's directions. Remove lid.

Stir apples. Mix cornstarch with water and stir into apples. Cook over medium-high heat, stirring often, 1 minute or until juices become clear and shiny. Makes 6 servings.

Variation

To make applesauce, spiced apples may be processed in a food processor, blender, or food mill until smooth.

Lemon Curd

This tangy English lemon curd is refreshing and delicious after a meal.
Served with blueberries or strawberries, it is pretty as well.

3 large eggs plus 1 egg yolk
1/4 cup butter, softened
3/4 cup fresh lemon juice

1 teaspoon grated lemon zest
1 1/3 cups superfine sugar
2 cups water

Butter 6 custard cups or ramekins.

Combine eggs, butter, lemon juice, lemon zest, and sugar in a bowl. Mix gently but thoroughly. Pour 1/2 cup of mixture into each cup. Cover with micro-proof plastic wrap or foil.

Pour water into pressure cooker. Insert steam basket. Place cups in basket, pyramid style, beginning with three cups at bottom. Secure lid. Over high heat, develop steam to medium-high pressure. Reduce heat to maintain pressure and cook 9 minutes. Release pressure according to manufacturer's directions. Remove lid.

Carefully remove cups to a wire rack. Remove plastic wrap. Using a tiny whisk or small fork, gently whisk filling. Refrigerate at least 4 hours. Serve chilled. Makes 6 servings.

Cook's Note: Superfine sugar can be easily made in the blender or food processor from regular granulated sugar.

Stuffed Apples with Rum Vanilla Sauce

*Serve apples with a dollop of ice cream or Chantilly Cream (page 158) and
Rum Vanilla Sauce (below) or drizzle with maple syrup.*

6 small baking apples
Stuffing (see below)
1 cup water

Stuffing:

1/2 cup toasted pecans (see Cook's Note,
  page 158)
1/2 cup raisins
1/3 cup toasted coconut (see Cook's Note,
  page 171)
1/4 cup butter, softened
1/4 cup firmly packed light brown sugar
Pinch of nutmeg

Rum Vanilla Sauce:

1/2 cup sugar
1 tablespoon cornstarch
1/4 cup water
1/4 cup half-and-half
1 teaspoon rum flavoring
2 egg yolks
2 tablespoons butter, softened

Core apples, leaving bottoms intact. Pierce peels with a cake tester or skewer in several places to prevent apples from splitting.

Prepare stuffing. Using a small spoon, fill apples with stuffing.

Pour water into pressure cooker. Layer apples in steam basket. Place in pressure cooker. Secure lid. Over high heat, develop steam to medium-high pressure. Reduce heat to maintain pressure and cook 8 minutes. Release pressure according to manufacturer's directions. Remove lid.

Remove basket from cooker and carefully transfer apples to a serving plate. Reserve cooking liquid to make Rum Vanilla Sauce. Prepare sauce and serve with apples. Makes 6 servings.

Stuffing

Combine pecans, raisins, coconut, butter, brown sugar, and nutmeg in a bowl. Mix thoroughly.

Rum Vanilla Sauce

In saucepan over high heat, dissolve sugar in reserved apple liquid. Dissolve cornstarch in water and stir into apple liquid. Cook, stirring, over medium-high heat until mixture begins to thicken.

Combine half-and-half, rum flavoring, egg yolks, and butter in a bowl. Mix thoroughly. Stir 1 tablespoon hot syrup into egg mixture, mix well, and pour egg mixture into syrup. Cook, stirring often, over medium-high heat until thickened.

Sauce may be rewarmed by simmering or in microwave oven on low power.

Cook's Notes: Apple corers are available at all fine cookshops. You may use a grapefruit knife and gently cut around core.

I prefer Michigan or Washington State apples. Select apples with a nice red color and no blemishes.

Chocolate Chocolate Chip Pudding

Just for chocolate lovers, this easy steamed pudding is served cold so it can be made ahead.

1/4 cup butter, softened
3/4 cup granulated sugar
1/4 cup firmly packed brown sugar
2 large eggs plus 1 egg yolk
2 tablespoons cornstarch
3 tablespoons cocoa powder

1 1/2 teaspoons vanilla extract
1 1/4 cups half-and-half
1/2 cup semisweet or milk chocolate chips
2 cups water
Chantilly Cream (page 158) to serve
Chocolate shavings to decorate

Butter bottom and sides of 6 ramekins or custard cups. Using an electric mixer, cream 1/4 cup butter and sugars together in a bowl 2 minutes. Add eggs, 1 at a time, and beat until well blended. Sift cornstarch and cocoa together. Gradually add to creamed mixture, beating thoroughly. Blend in vanilla and half-and-half.

Pour a scant 1/2 cup cocoa batter into each prepared cup. Top each with heaping tablespoon of chocolate chips. Cover each cup with foil.

Pour water into pressure cooker. Place steam basket in cooker. Arrange cups, pyramid style, in basket, beginning with three cups at bottom. Secure lid. Over high heat, develop steam to medium-high pressure. Reduce heat to maintain pressure and cook 9 minutes. Release pressure according to manufacturer's directions. Remove lid.

Remove covered custard cups and place on wire rack to cool. Remove foil. Refrigerate 4 to 6 hours. Serve with dollops of Chantilly Cream and shaved chocolate. Makes 6 to 8 servings.

Creamy Honey Rice Pudding

Long- or short-grain rice may be used in this creamy dessert that is flavored with orange zest and spices.

1 cup white rice
2 1/4 cups water
1 (2-inch piece) orange peel
1 (2- to 3-inch) cinnamon stick
1/2 teaspoon salt
1/8 teaspoon freshly ground nutmeg
2 tablespoons butter

1/4 cup honey
1/2 cup sugar
3/4 cup half-and-half
3 large egg yolks
1/2 cup golden raisins
1/2 teaspoon vanilla extract
Ground cinnamon

In a pressure cooker, combine rice, water, orange peel, cinnamon stick, salt, and nutmeg. Secure lid. Over high heat, develop steam to high pressure. Reduce heat to maintain pressure and cook 8 minutes. Release pressure according to manufacturer's directions. Remove lid.

Add butter, honey, and sugar to rice mixture. Gently stir with fork. Remove cinnamon stick and orange peel. Beat half-and-half and egg yolks together in a bowl. Add to rice mixture and cook over medium-high heat 3 minutes or until mixture comes to a simmer. Stir in raisins and vanilla.

Spoon pudding into individual serving dishes and sprinkle with cinnamon. Makes 6 to 8 servings.

Variation

In the Middle East, rice pudding is flavored with rosewater instead of vanilla.

Festive Italian Cheesecake

This festive and colorful Italian cheesecake is traditionally served during the holidays.
The mascarpone cheese, made from cow's milk, is from Lombardy, Italy,
and is double-rich in cream. It is found in specialty food stores or Italian markets.

Double Almond Crust (see below)
1 (3-oz.) package almond paste, crumbled
1 (15-oz.) carton ricotta cheese, at room temperature
2 (4-oz.) packages mascarpone cheese, softened
1/2 teaspoon grated lemon zest
2 large eggs, at room temperature
1 cup powdered sugar, sifted
1/4 teaspoon ground nutmeg

1 teaspoon almond extract
1/3 cup chopped candied fruit
1/2 cup semisweet chocolate chips
1 cup water

Double Almond Crust:

1 cup ground toasted almonds
3 ounces almond paste
2 tablespoons sugar
1 tablespoon butter, softened

Prepare crust. Set aside. Using an electric mixer, beat almond paste, cheeses, and lemon zest together 1 minute. Beat in eggs, one at a time. Add sugar, nutmeg, and almond extract. Mix thoroughly. Carefully fold in fruit and chocolate chips.

Pour batter into crust. Place 2 layers of paper towels over top of pan, top with foil, and crimp along edge of pan to seal. Place into the center of a foil harness (page 175).

Pour water into pressure cooker. Insert steam basket. Place pan in basket. Loop top of harness into a handle. Secure lid. Over high heat, develop steam to high pressure. Reduce heat to maintain pressure and cook 25 minutes. Release pressure according to manufacturer's directions. Remove lid.

Remove pan and place on wire rack. Refrigerate overnight or at least 4 hours. Makes 6 to 8 servings.

Double Almond Crust

Combine almonds, paste, sugar, and butter in a small bowl. Mix thoroughly. Press crumbs evenly into a 7-inch springform pan (see Cook's Note below), covering bottom and 1 inch of sides.

Cook's Note: Seven-inch springform pans are found in specialty cookshops. If, however, your pressure cooker comes with a steam basket, line it with micro-proof plastic wrap or foil and use the basket as a pan.

Fudgy Peanut Butter Cheesecake

What could be better than peanut butter and chocolate?
This creamy peanutty cheesecake will be favored by all!

Peanut Crust (see opposite)
1 cup peanut butter
2 (8-oz.) packages cream cheese, softened
1/2 cup firmly packed light brown sugar
1/2 cup powdered sugar, sifted
2 tablespoons cornstarch
2 large eggs
1/4 cup sour cream
1 (12-oz.) package semisweet chocolate chips, melted

2 cups water
Whipped cream to decorate
Chocolate curls to decorate

Peanut Crust:

1 cup ground toasted unsalted peanuts (see Cook's Note, page 158)
1/4 cup firmly packed brown sugar
1 tablespoon unsweetened cocoa powder
3 tablespoons butter, melted

Prepare crust. Set aside. Using an electric mixer, blend peanut butter, cheese, sugars, and cornstarch together in a bowl until smooth. Beat in eggs, 1 at a time, and blend in sour cream. Pour in melted chocolate and blend on low speed until thoroughly mixed. Pour batter into crust. Cover with 2 layers of paper towels, top with foil, and crimp along edge to seal.

Pour water into pressure cooker. Insert steam basket. Prepare foil harness (page 175). Place pan in harness and lower into cooker. Loop top of harness into a handle. Secure lid. Over high heat, develop steam to high pressure. Reduce heat to maintain pressure and cook 22 minutes. Release pressure according to manufacturer's directions. Remove lid. Lift pan from cooker and place on wire rack. Refrigerate at least 4 hours. Remove cover.

Decorate with whipped cream and chocolate curls. Makes 6 to 8 servings.

Peanut Crust

Combine peanuts, brown sugar, cocoa, and butter in a small bowl. Press into a 7-inch springform pan, covering bottom and 1 inch of sides.

Cook's Note: The unsalted peanuts are available at supermarkets.

Lemon Cheesecake

Almonds and lemon are a delight together, as in this lemon-flavored cheesecake with an almond crust.

Almond Crust (see opposite)
2 (8-oz.) packages cream cheese, softened
1 1/3 cups powdered sugar, sifted
1 teaspoon grated lemon zest
2 tablespoons cornstarch
2 large eggs, at room temperature
1/3 cup fresh lemon juice
1 cup water

Almond Crust:
1 cup toasted blanched almonds, ground
3 tablespoons granulated sugar
3 tablespoons butter, melted
Dash of nutmeg

Prepare crust. Set aside. Using an electric mixer, blend cream cheese, powdered sugar, lemon zest, and cornstarch together in a bowl 1 minute. Beat in eggs, 1 at a time, beating thoroughly after each addition. Drizzle lemon juice into creamed mixture and beat at low speed until blended.

Pour batter into crust. Cover with 2 layers of paper towels, top with foil, and crimp along edge to seal. Pour water into pressure cooker. Insert steam rack. Prepare foil harness (page 175). Place pan in harness, folding top of harness into a handle, and lower into cooker. Secure lid. Over high heat, develop steam to high pressure. Reduce heat to maintain pressure and cook 22 minutes. Release pressure according to manufacturer's directions. Remove lid.

Remove cheesecake and place on wire rack. Refrigerate at least 4 hours. Remove cover. Serve chilled. Blueberries are great with this cheesecake. Makes 6 to 8 servings.

Almond Crust

Combine almonds, sugar, butter, and nutmeg in mixing bowl. Blend thoroughly. Press into a 7-inch springform pan, covering bottom and 1 inch of sides. Set aside.

Cook's Note: Lemon zest is the yellow outer skin of the lemon, grated off with a traditional grater or with a gadget called a lemon zester. Be careful, however, not to dig into the white layer under the yellow skin. It will give a bitter flavor.

Pumpkin Cheesecake

This autumn dessert is a favorite, filled with all the lovely spicy flavors of the season.
You'll love the cinnamon added to the whipped cream topping.

Pecan Crust (see opposite)
2 (8-oz.) packages cream cheese, softened
1 1/4 cups powdered sugar
1 teaspoon grated orange peel
2 large eggs, at room temperature
1 cup canned pumpkin
2 tablespoons butter, softened
3 tablespoons cornstarch
1 teaspoon ground cinnamon
1/2 teaspoon ground nutmeg
1/8 teaspoon ground ginger
1 cup water
Spiced Whipped Cream (see opposite)

Pecan Crust:

1/2 cup graham cracker crumbs
1/3 cup granulated sugar
1/2 cup toasted pecans, finely chopped (see
   Cook's Note, page 158)
1/2 teaspoon cinnamon
1/4 cup butter, melted

Spiced Whipped Cream:

1 cup whipping cream
3 tablespoons powdered sugar
1/8 teaspoon ground cinnamon

Prepare crust. Set aside. Using an electric mixer, beat cream cheese, sugar, and orange peel together 1 minute. Beat in eggs, 1 at a time, beating thoroughly after each addition. Beat in pumpkin, butter, cornstarch, cinnamon, nutmeg, and ginger, beating just until smooth.

Pour batter over crust. Cover with 2 layers of paper towels, top with foil, and crimp along edge of pan to seal.

Pour water into pressure cooker. Insert steam basket. Prepare foil harness (page 175). Place pan in harness, lower into cooker, and loop top of harness into a handle. Secure lid. Over high heat, develop steam to high pressure. Reduce heat to maintain pressure and cook 25 minutes. Release pressure according to manufacturer's directions. Remove lid.

Lift cheesecake from cooker and place on wire rack. Refrigerate at least 3 hours. Remove cover. Prepare Spiced Whipped Cream and serve with cheesecake. Makes 6 servings.

Pecan Crust

Combine crumbs, sugar, pecans, cinnamon, and butter in a small bowl. Press crumbs into bottom of 7-inch springform pan.

Spiced Whipped Cream

Using an electric mixer, beat cream in a medium-size bowl until it begins to thicken. Add powdered sugar and cinnamon and whip until thickened.

Dried Fruit Compote

*Serve this wonderfully delicious compote in winter when good fresh fruit is unavailable.
It makes a wonderful breakfast dish or light dessert.*

---

1 cup golden raisins
1 (8-oz.) package dried apricots
1 (8-oz.) package dried peaches
1 1/2 cups orange juice

2/3 cup sugar
1 cinnamon stick
4 whole cloves

In a pressure cooker, combine fruit, orange juice, sugar, and spices. Secure lid. Over high heat, develop steam to high pressure. Reduce heat to maintain pressure and cook 3 minutes. Release pressure according to manufacturer's directions. Remove lid. Continue cooking over medium heat 2 more minutes, stirring occasionally.

Store in a covered bowl in the refrigerator up to 1 week. Makes 6 servings.

South Pacific Bread Pudding with Pineapple Sauce

The tropical flavors of coconut and pineapple are refreshing and delicious.

1 (16-oz.) can cream of coconut
1 cup half-and-half
3 large eggs, beaten
1/2 cup butter, melted
3/4 cup sugar
1 1/2 teaspoons rum flavoring
1/4 teaspoon grated nutmeg
1 (20-oz.) can pineapple chunks, drained and juice reserved
1 1/4 cups toasted coconut (see Cook's Note opposite), divided
8 cups (2-inch cubes) Italian or French bread
1 1/2 cups water

Pineapple Sauce:
1/4 cup butter
3/4 cup sugar
1 (20-oz.) can crushed pineapple, undrained, plus reserved pineapple juice from pudding recipe, to measure 3 cups
1/2 teaspoon orange zest
1 tablespoon plus 2 teaspoons cornstarch mixed with 1/4 cup pineapple juice

Butter an 8-inch round baking pan or steam basket from pressure cooker (see Appendix). If using steam basket, cover outside of basket with foil.

Combine cream of coconut, half-and-half, eggs, butter, sugar, rum flavoring, and nutmeg in a bowl. Beat thoroughly. Mix in pineapple and 1 cup coconut. Place bread in a large bowl. Pour creamed mixture over bread. Toss until bread is well moistened and mixed. Spoon mixture into prepared pan or basket.

Pour water into pressure cooker. Prepare foil harness (page 175). Place pan in harness and lower into cooker. If using basket, place a metal measuring cup in bottom of cooker and set steam basket, filled with bread pudding, on measuring cup.

Secure lid. Over high heat, develop steam to high pressure. Reduce heat to maintain pressure and cook 12 minutes. Release pressure according to manufacturer's directions. Remove lid.

Remove pan from cooker and place on wire rack to cool. Sprinkle with remaining coconut. Prepare Pineapple Sauce. Serve pudding warm, or chilled with sauce. Makes 6 to 8 servings.

Pineapple Sauce

In a saucepan, combine butter, sugar, pineapple, 3 cups pineapple juice, and orange zest. Mix well and bring to a boil. Stir cornstarch mixture and add to pineapple mixture. Cook, stirring, until thickened. Great as an ice cream topping, too!

Cook's Notes: To toast coconut, scatter evenly on a baking sheet. Preheat oven to 375°F (190°C). Bake 4 minutes or until golden brown.

The quality of the bread is extremely important in all bread pudding recipes and should not be overlooked.

Fresh Pear Cups with Zabaglione Cream & Raspberries

This delicate dessert is Italian in origin and deliciously beautiful to serve. Select firm pears, free of blemishes and soft spots. The Bosc pear works very well in this recipe— it has a sweet-tart flavor and holds its shape while cooking.

6 ripe pears, peeled
1/2 cup pear liqueur or Grand Marnier
1/4 cup water
1 cup sugar
4 large egg yolks

1/3 cup half-and-half or milk
2 teaspoons cornstarch
2 cups fresh raspberries or blueberries
2 tablespoons raspberry liqueur

Cut pears in halves horizontally (crosswise). Remove core and some pulp from bottom halves, leaving bottoms intact and sides 1/2 inch thick. Pear bottoms should resemble small cups. Eat pear tops or discard.

In a pressure cooker, combine pear liqueur, water, sugar and pear bottoms. Secure lid. Over high heat, develop steam to high pressure. Reduce heat to maintain pressure and cook 4 minutes. Release pressure according to manufacturer's directions. Remove lid.

Using a slotted spoon, transfer pear cups to a serving dish.

Whisk egg yolks in a small bowl. Whisk 1/4 cup hot pear liquid into egg yolks, then pour egg mixture into liquid in cooker. Cook over medium heat, stirring frequently, until thickened and bubbles disappear. Add half-and-half and cornstarch. Cook, stirring, 2 minutes or until thickened.

Spoon sauce into pear cups. Cover with plastic wrap and refrigerate. Combine raspberries and raspberry liqueur. Serve with raspberries sprinkled over filled pears. Makes 6 servings.

Steamed Christmas Pudding

Forget about hours and hours of steaming Christmas pudding. This family favorite is completed in less than half the time, and the result is a pudding with a delicate, delicious texture and flavor that will delight everyone.

1 cup toasted pecans, coarsely chopped (see Cook's Note, page 158)
1 cup candied red or green cherries
1/2 cup currants
1/2 cup mixed candied fruit
1 1/2 cups all-purpose flour, divided
1/2 cup corn oil
1 1/2 cups powdered sugar, sifted
2 teaspoons grated orange zest
2 eggs
2 teaspoons baking powder
1 teaspoon ground cinnamon
1/2 teaspoon ground allspice
1/2 teaspoon grated nutmeg

3 tablespoons orange liqueur
1/4 cup molasses
3 cups water
Orange Vanilla Sauce (optional) (see below)

Orange Vanilla Sauce:

1 1/2 cups milk
1 cup sugar
2 tablespoons cornstarch
3 tablespoons butter
2 tablespoons orange liqueur
1 teaspoon vanilla extract
1 egg yolk

Combine pecans and fruit in a large bowl. Sprinkle with 1/2 cup flour, tossing until fruit is thoroughly coated. Set aside. Using an electric mixer, beat oil, powdered sugar, and orange zest together 1 minute. Beat in eggs, 1 at a time, beating well after each addition. Combine remaining 1 cup flour, baking powder, and spices in a small bowl. Alternately add liqueur and dry ingredients to egg mixture, beating well. Beat in molasses. Fold batter into fruit.

Spray a 6-cup tubular steamed pudding mold with nonstick cooking spray. Pour batter into mold. Tap mold several times on work surface and seal with lid of the mold or cover with foil.

Pour water into pressure cooker. Insert steam basket. Lower pudding mold into basket. Secure lid. Over high heat, develop steam to high pressure. Reduce heat to maintain pressure and cook 50 minutes. Open steam vent. Increase heat to medium and cook 20 minutes. Release pressure according to manufacturer's directions. Remove lid.

Remove pudding mold and place on a wire rack to cool. Let stand 15 minutes. Wrap in cheesecloth soaked in bourbon. Seal in foil. Store in a cool, dry place up to 2 months or at least 24 hours.

Invert on a round serving platter. Prepare Orange Vanilla Sauce, if using. Serve with sauce. Makes 8 to 12 servings.

Orange Vanilla Sauce

In a saucepan, combine milk, sugar, cornstarch, and butter. Cook over medium-high heat, stirring often, until mixture begins to thicken.

Whisk liqueur, vanilla, and egg yolk together in a bowl. Pour 1/4 cup hot milk mixture into yolk mixture and blend together. Whisk yolk mixture into milk mixture and cook over medium heat, stirring, until it begins to bubble.

Cook's Notes: The fruit is coated with flour at the beginning so when added to the rest of the ingredients, the flour enables the fruit to attach to the batter and not sink to the bottom of the pan.

To flame the pudding tableside, heat 2 tablespoons 80 percent bourbon. Place 2 sugar cubes in center of pudding in a tiny flameproof container. Pour heated bourbon over sugar cubes and ignite.

Blueberry Bread Pudding

*Serve pudding hot or cold with a dollop of Chantilly Cream (page 158), ice cream,
or warm milk poured over the top.*

1/2 cup butter, melted
1 cup half-and-half or milk
1 1/2 cups sugar
2 large eggs, lightly beaten
1 teaspoon vanilla extract

1/2 teaspoon ground nutmeg
2 cups blueberries
8 cups (2-inch cubes) Italian or French bread
1 1/2 cups water

Butter an 8-inch round baking pan or steam basket from pressure cooker (see Appendix). If using steam basket, line basket, cover outside of basket with foil.

Combine butter, half-and-half, sugar, eggs, vanilla, and nutmeg in a bowl. Beat until smooth. Stir in blueberries. Place bread cubes into a large bowl. Pour fruit mixture over bread cubes. Toss until bread is well moistened. Spoon mixture into prepared pan.

Pour water into pressure cooker. Insert steam rack. Prepare foil harness (page 175). Place pan in center of harness, lower into cooker, and loop top of harness into a handle. Secure lid. Over high heat, develop steam to high pressure. Reduce heat to maintain pressure and cook 15 minutes. Release pressure according to manufacturer's directions. Remove lid. Lift pan from cooker and place on wire rack to cool. Makes 6 to 8 servings.

Variation

The pudding may be prepared with fresh or frozen blueberries. If frozen blueberries are used, drain excess liquid after defrosting.

HARNESS FOR REMOVING PANS FROM PRESSURE COOKER

A harness made of foil strips is extremely useful in transferring pans or other dessert containers into and out of the pressure cooker.

- Tear a 30-inch length of foil. Cut in half lengthwise. Fold each strip into thirds lengthwise.

- Crisscross the two folded strips and tape at the center to secure.

- Set pan or container in center of crossed strips, bring ends together over top of pan or container, and fold to secure.

Chutneys & Jams

Chutneys are composed of a variety of fruits and vegetables. Explore chutney flavors by taking the combinations beyond conventional components: try plums, squash, tomatoes, and berries adding zest with garlic, chives, peppercorns, and mustard.

Select unblemished fresh fruit and vegetables. When using dried fruit in a recipe calling for fresh fruit, increase the liquid by 1 cup for each pound of dried fruit.

Always use cooking utensils of nonreactive materials such as ceramic, stainless steel, or enamel for cooking mixtures containing vinegar.

Serve chutneys hot or cold with meat, poultry, rice, or casseroles. Chutneys also add flavor to stuffings.

Blueberry Pecan Chutney

Blueberry Pecan Chutney may be prepared in season with fresh berries or frozen blueberries may be used if fresh blueberries aren't available. Drain excess fluid from defrosted blueberries before using. This chutney is delicious with roast pork. The ginger and cayenne add a spicy flavor.

1 1/2 cups pecan pieces, toasted (see Cook's Note, page 158)
1 1/2 pounds blueberries
1 cup raisins
2 small red onions, sliced
3/4 cup orange marmalade
1 tablespoon lemon zest
1/4 cup orange juice
1/4 cup lemon juice

1/2 cup white wine
1 1/2 cups sugar
1/2 teaspoon salt
1/2 teaspoon red (cayenne) pepper
1 teaspoon ground ginger
1 bay leaf
1 cinnamon stick

In a pressure cooker, combine pecans, blueberries, raisins, onions, marmalade, lemon zest, orange juice, lemon juice, wine, sugar, salt, and spices. Stir well. Secure lid. Over high heat, develop steam to medium pressure. Reduce heat to maintain pressure and cook 3 minutes. Release pressure according to manufacturer's directions. Remove lid.

Remove bay leaf and cinnamon stick. Stir chutney thoroughly.

Pour hot chutney into a sterilized jar with lid. Store airtight in refrigerator up to 3 to 4 weeks. Makes 6 cups.

Cranberry Chutney

A family favorite, I share this with everyone, especially at holiday time when cranberries are available. Bottled with a colorful bow around the top, the chutney makes a welcome hostess gift that everyone raves about.

1 1/2 cups walnut pieces, toasted (see Cook's Note, page 158)
1 pound cranberries
1 cup golden raisins
1 small red onion, sliced
1/2 cup orange marmalade
1/2 cup orange juice
2 tablespoons orange zest
1/3 cup white wine vinegar

1 cup granulated sugar
1/2 cup firmly packed brown sugar
1/2 teaspoon salt
1/4 teaspoon red (cayenne) pepper
1/2 teaspoon ground ginger
1 cinnamon stick
1 bay leaf

In a pressure cooker, combine walnuts, cranberries, raisins, onion, marmalade, orange juice, zest, vinegar, sugars, salt, and spices. Stir well. Secure lid. Over high heat, develop steam to medium pressure. Reduce heat to maintain pressure and cook 5 minutes. Release pressure according to manufacturer's directions. Remove lid.

Remove cinnamon stick and bay leaf from chutney. Stir well.

Pour hot chutney into a sterilized jar with lid. Store airtight in refrigerator up to 3 to 4 weeks. Makes 8 cups.

Blueberry Jam

Make this delicious jam when blueberries are at their peak. I learned to add the ribbon to the paraffin from my mother. It acts as a lifter when you are ready to remove the paraffin.

4 cups blueberries
4 cups sugar
1 cup orange juice
1 teaspoon grated orange peel

1/2 teaspoon grated nutmeg
1 (6-oz.) bottle pectin or 1 (1 3/4-oz.)
   package dry pectin
Melted paraffin

In a pressure cooker, combine blueberries, sugar, orange juice, orange peel, and nutmeg. Stir well. Secure lid. Over high heat, develop steam to medium pressure. Reduce heat to maintain pressure and cook 2 minutes. Release pressure according to manufacturer's directions. Remove lid.

Stir blueberry mixture well. Process in a food mill, over a bowl, separating skins from pulp. Return pulp to pressure cooker. Over high heat, stir pectin into pulp and bring to a rolling boil. Cook, stirring with a long-handled wooden spoon, 1 minute.

Ladle jam into 8 sterilized 1/2-pint jars, filling to 1 inch below rim and being careful not to splash on rim or upper inch of jar. Use damp cloth to wipe rim and inside of jar.

Pour melted paraffin over jam. Insert both ends of a 5-inch length of ribbon in center of each paraffin cover. Set aside undisturbed for 24 hours. Store airtight in refrigerator up to 3 to 4 weeks.

Blueberry jam may also be frozen in freezer containers for 6 to 8 months. Makes 8 (1/2 pints).

Ginger Pear Jam

Use your favorite pears, selecting ripe pears that are free of blemishes or dark spots.

2 1/2 pounds pears, peeled, cored, and thinly
  sliced
4 cups sugar
1/2 cup orange juice

1 teaspoon grated ginger root
1 (6-oz.) bottle pectin
Melted paraffin

In a pressure cooker, combine pears, sugar, orange juice, and ginger. Stir well. Secure lid. Over high heat, develop steam to high pressure. Reduce heat to maintain pressure and cook 6 minutes. Release pressure according to manufacturer's directions. Remove lid.

Using a slotted spoon, transfer pears to a food processor, blender, or food mill. Process until coarsely pureed. Return to pressure cooker. Cook pear mixture over medium heat 1 minute. Stir in pectin and bring to a full boil. Cook 1 minute, stirring with a long-handled wooden spoon to avoid being splattered by bubbling mixture.

Remove from heat. Ladle into 8 sterilized 1/2-pint jars, filling to 1 inch below top. Avoid dripping pear mixture on rim or upper inch of jar. Use a damp cloth to wipe away any pear mixture or juice on rim or inside of jar.

Pour melted paraffin on jam. Insert both ends of 5-inch length of ribbon in center of each paraffin cover. Set aside undisturbed 24 hours. Store airtight in refrigerator up to 3 to 4 weeks.

Pear jam may be frozen in freezer containers 6 to 8 months. Makes 8 (1/2 pints).

Peach-Apricot Preserves with Almonds

The toasted almonds add a nutty flavor that comes from the oils during the toasting process. When combined with the flavor of the apricots and peaches, it makes a delightfully flavored topping for toast.

6 whole fresh peaches
1 cup water
1 (8-oz.) package dried apricots, chopped
1/2 cup almonds, toasted (see Cook's Note, page 158), coarsely chopped
1 1/2 cups orange juice

4 1/2 cups sugar
2 whole cloves
1 cinnamon stick
1 (1 3/4-oz.) package pectin powder
Melted paraffin

Pierce peaches with cake tester or skewer. Pour water into a pressure cooker. Place peaches in water. Secure lid. Over high heat, develop steam to high pressure. Reduce heat to maintain pressure and cook 3 minutes. Release pressure according to manufacturer's directions. Remove lid. Place peaches into a bowl filled with cold water. Peel peaches. Slice peaches into wedges.

In a pressure cooker, combine peaches, apricots, almonds, orange juice, sugar, cloves, and cinnamon. Stir well. Secure lid. Over high heat, develop steam to medium pressure. Reduce heat to maintain pressure and cook 2 minutes. Release pressure according to manufacturer's directions. Remove lid.

Stir fruit mixture thoroughly. Remove cloves and cinnamon stick. Sprinkle pectin over fruit and stir well. Cook over medium-high heat 2 minutes.

Ladle preserves into 8 sterilized 1/2-pint jars, filling to 1 inch below rim. Be careful to avoid splashing preserves on rim. Preserves may be covered and frozen. If not freezing, carefully pour melted paraffin over preserves. Insert both ends of 5-inch length of ribbon in center of paraffin cover. Set aside undisturbed for 24 hours. Store airtight in refrigerator up to 3 to 4 weeks. Makes 8 (1/2 pints).

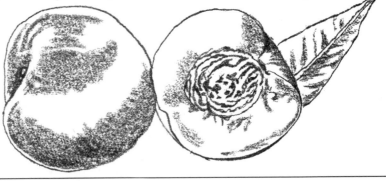

Appendix

Understanding the Pressure Cooker

The first generation pressure cookers popular in the thirties and forties were complicated, had many parts to deal with, and lacked safety features. We've all heard the horror stories our grandmothers and mothers told about using the older models. Technology has advanced by leaps and bounds since then. The new generation of pressure cookers introduced to the public since 1985 offers easy-to-use equipment without the hassle of feeling like you must be an engineer instead of a cook. The new-generation pressure cookers and their lids offer safety features including a system where extra steam escapes, preventing any accidents. The new-generation pressure cooker is perfectly safe and the new materials used in construction seal the steam under the lid, penetrating the food fibers and resulting in extremely quick and delicious meals.

The newly designed lids allow very little steam to escape. This means less liquid is required to pressure cook, helping retain nutrients during the cooking process.

Combining and layering courses is easy and can be accomplished in a pressure cooker with excellent results. Simply refer to the timing charts. Plan to cook compatible foods. Interrupting the pressure cooking process can easily be done. Meats take longer than vegetables. Pressure cook the meat first, interrupting the cooking process to add the vegetables for the last few minutes.

It has long been recognized that the pressure cooker is a great energy saver. During World War II, when energy was necessarily conserved, it was the pressure cooker that prepared most home-cooked meals. As much as 60 to 70 percent of the time is saved, and the shorter cooking time cuts the consumption of energy by two-thirds. Today, with rising gas and electricity costs, it is a sensible alternative to save dollars in the household budget.

Selecting the Right Pressure Cooker

Even though the principles of pressure cooking remain the same, there are great variations in the craftsmanship and materials of the various models. Deluxe, standard, large, and small pressure cookers are available in the marketplace. The six-quart pressure cooker is the industry standard, and all the recipes in this book can be prepared in it. Pressure cookers vary in construction, type of metal, and accessories. Everything should be considered and examined before the initial purchase is made.

Pressure cookers are constructed of either aluminum, enamel-coated carbon steel, or stainless steel metals. Even though aluminum is known for fine heat conduction, the stainless steel or enamel-coated carbon steel should seriously be considered because there is no interaction between these metals and the foods. Aluminum will darken when in contact with acidic foods such as tomatoes or citrus products and a metallic taste will penetrate the food. Look for a pressure cooker of heavy-gauge metal, with an easy-to-clean surface and interior. Preferably, the handles should be constructed of heat-proof material and include a helping handle on the opposite side for easy lifting.

All it takes is a little preplanning. Remember, quality will indeed endure long after the price is forgotten.

Features of the Pressure Cooker

Pressure valves: Always review the manufacturer's manual first. Examine the construction of the unit. Is the pressure valve secure and built into the lid, or is it a free-standing plug that balances on top of the lid? The well-constructed pressure cooker has pressure valves that are attached to the lid with gauge lines to indicate the various pressures. Look for a well-designed, easy-to-read gauge that can be disassembled for thorough cleaning. The wobbly, balancing plugs may cause difficulty in determining when the exact pressure level has been reached. Amount of pressure and timing are key factors to pressure cooking success.

The new pressure cookers have technically improved valves that will not explode. They are designed so the excess steam will escape before a disaster can occur! Forget about the horror stories of the 1940s.

Rubber seal ring: The rubber ring around the lid plays a very important part in the functioning of the pressure cooker. Double-check the rubber ring for firmness, cracks, or peeling. It should be smooth and fit snugly. It can easily be removed for cleaning and should be washed thoroughly and rubbed with mineral oil after every use. The oil will preserve the ring, and properly cared for, the ring should last for approximately 150 meals. It is a good idea to have a spare rubber ring on hand. They are available from the merchant where the pressure cooker was purchased, or write to the manufacturer. Address and parts information will be found in the manual.

When should the rubber ring seal be changed? The steam pressure will not develop and you will see the steam flow from around the edge of the lid. When this happens, double-check the ring for cleanliness. Remove any food particles that may have adhered to the seal. Check positioning of the lid. Is it sealed correctly? If all of these have been checked thoroughly and everything seems to be in order, your next step would be to replace the rubber ring seal.

Pressure release: Many units offer a pressure/steam escape button near the valve. There will be times when the pressure should be adjusted during cooking, and this is when you will most appreciate the convenience of the steam escape button, which may be used instead of transferring the pressure cooker to the sink so cold water can be run over the cooker to release the steam or reduce pressure for delicate foods. The button release is an extremely useful feature.

Steam basket: Found packed with most units, the steam basket is great for fresh vegetables, fruit, or fish. It is designed with elevated feet to keep the unit away from the liquid and has little holes for steam penetration and circulation.

Heat diffuser: A heat diffuser is a wire or metal plate that prevents direct contact between the heat and the bottom of the pressure cooker. Most manufacturers include a heat diffuser with the pressure cooker. If, however, it is not a part of the package, they can be found in most cookshops very inexpensively. Heat diffusers should be used when preparing all rice, pasta, or bean recipes. It prevents sticking and scorching.

Cake pans or pudding molds: Many times a recipe will call for a cake pan, pudding mold, or tart pan. These should be made of any heatproof material, such as metal or tempered glass.

Timer: A timer won't come with the pressure cooker, but it should. It is important that all recipes be accurately timed, so purchase a good-quality timer.

Pressure Cooking Terms

Lock the lid into place: First and foremost, read the manufacturer's manual carefully. Most units have symbols on the lid handle and the vessel handle. Once these symbols are lined up, the lid slips into the proper position and is secured in place. Practice positioning the lid and locking it into place several times until confidence is developed before starting to cook.

Secure the lid: Align the lid with the lower part of the vessel and lock it into position.

Develop pressure: Bring the pressure up to the level indicated in the recipe.

Release the steam: Releasing steam can be done in three ways.

Rapid release is great for vegetables or fish dishes. Carefully carry the pressure cooker to the sink, release the lock as the manufacturer directs, and run cold water over the top of the lid.

The steam release latch or button works well for soups and stews. This handy addition to the newer units allows the steam to escape without transferring the vessel to the sink. Simply unlock the latch and release the steam until all pressurized steam has escaped. The lid will easily open.

Slow release is simply sliding the cooker off the burner and allowing it to stand until the cooker cools, releasing the pressure. This slow process usually takes 15 minutes or so, affecting the texture of the food. It is not a recommended method; the extra cooking time causes foods to overcook.

Precaution: If the pressure cooker is left unattended after the cooking time is completed, the lid can form a seal and it will be impossible to release the lid. Simply put the pressure cooker back on the heat and bring the pressure up to low. Then, release the steam and the lid can be removed. Redeveloping the pressure breaks the seal.

Remove the lid: The lids on the new pressure cookers will not come off until all pressure is released. It is important to read the manufacturer's manual for instructions on properly removing the lid. Practice a few times, adding a cup of water to the pressure cooker, developing pressure, releasing the pressure, and removing the lid.

Adjust heat to maintain pressure: Once the desired pressure has been reached, it is important to reduce the heat to medium or lower to maintain the pressure at the correct level. Because the heating units of cook tops vary, it will be necessary to keep adjusting the heat until the correct amount is achieved.

Slide heat diffuser between pan and heat: The heat diffuser (page 185) prevents scorching and burning, especially while preparing starchy rices or pastas. The heat diffuser should be put over the burner after pressure has been reached.

Interrupting the process: This method is used most often when ingredients requiring long periods of cooking are combined with ingredients that require shorter cooking periods. Pressure is released quickly, usually under cold, running water, and the lid is removed. At this point, the second batch of ingredients is added for the last few minutes of cooking, ensuring perfect results and texture. The lid is secured into position and the cooking time completed. The pressure is once again released and the lid removed.

Amount of liquid: The manufacturer's manual will recommend a minimum amount of liquid for the pressure cooker. Never use less than recommended. The liquid is the key to developing the steam that creates the pressure under the tightly fitting lid. The magic of pressure cooking develops when the water is heated to above boiling (212°F, 100°C) temperatures. The pressure continues to climb under the tightly sealed lid and is measured by pounds of pressure thereafter and will be indicated on the valve gauge of the pressure cooker or a weight that is added to the exhaust valve of the pressure cooker. The deluxe pressure cookers' gauges have lines that appear as the steam rises. Standard models create steam and jiggle the gauge at a slow, even pace.

Amount of pressure: Low pressure is developed when steam under the sealed lid is around 220°F (105°C). Low steam pressure is used for custards, puddings, and delicate fruit and vegetables. As the steam develops under the sealed lid, the pressure continues to increase, unless the heat is reduced to adjust the steam.

Medium pressure is developed when steam reaches 235°F (115°C) and is recommended for poultry, fish, and some firmer fruits and vegetables.

High pressure is developed at about 250°F (120°C), which again is indicated by lines on the deluxe units and a rapid jiggling of the gauge on the standard models. High pressure is recommended for tough cuts of meat, wild game, dried fruits, firm fruits and vegetables, beans, rice, and pasta.
High-altitude cooking: Above 3,500 feet, always increase cooking time by 10 percent.

Pressure	Pounds	Temperature
High	15	250°F (120°C)
Medium	10	235°F (115°C)
Low	5	220°F (105°C)

LET'S PRESSURE COOK

1. Make sure the manual has been read and is understood.
2. Examine ring and seal on unit.
3. Read selected recipe thoroughly.
4. Organize ingredients and prepare as required.
5. Use proper measuring utensils. Check liquid measurements at eye level. Loosely pack dry ingredients and level off straight across top with a spatula.
6. All recipes in this cookbook were tested in a 6-quart pressure cooker.
7. Regardless of whether there are one or four people in the family, it is recommended that you prepare the entire recipe. Leftovers can easily be frozen in portioned packages and enjoyed at a later time.

EIGHT STEPS FOR PERFECT PRESSURE COOKING

1. Always read the manufacturer's manual thoroughly so you will understand each part. Have on hand spare rubber rings. Always double-check the flexibility of the valve.
2. Read recipe through. Does the recipe fit the unit? Meat, poultry, or fish pieces must be of same thickness. Trim fat from meat and cut all vegetables the same size. Assemble all ingredients for the recipe before starting to cook.
3. Use more, never less, liquid as required by the manufacturer. Tomato sauce, stocks, and juices are all considered liquid. Oil is not included.
4. Use a heat diffuser on the range burner when cooking rice, pasta, or beans.
5. Secure lid according to manufacturer's directions and develop pressure. Once pressure is reached, timing begins. Adjust heat to maintain pressure.
6. Invest in an accurate timer. It is as crucial as developing the pressure.
7. Follow manual instructions to cool pressure down. For quick steam release, run the unit under cold water or release and press the pressure release button. When preparing soups and stocks, the pressure is best released slowly. Once pressure is released, shake the unit several times before removing the lid. The shaking adjusts the inner temperature.

   If the lid is left on long after pressure is gone, a seal will form. To release the lid, develop low pressure over low heat once again. Release steam rapidly and remove lid.
8. Thoroughly cleanse the unit in hot, sudsy water. Make sure the valve area is thoroughly clean. Remove the rubber ring and wash with sudsy water. Rinse, dry, and rub mineral oil all over rubber surface. This extra step adds endurance to the ring. The rings last for approximately 150 uses. Store unit with lid inverted, not locked into position.

CONVERTING YOUR FAVORITE RECIPE

1. Separate ingredients according to length of pressure cooking time (see charts in each chapter).
2. Make sure all ingredients are cut into uniform pieces.
3. If cooking a soup or stew, sear meat or poultry to seal in juices.
4. Add the minimum liquid required for your unit. This includes stocks, tomato puree or sauces, water, or juices.
5. Begin cooking meat or poultry first until almost completely cooked (see timing chart for meat, page 57).
6. Interrupt cooking process by releasing steam according to manufacturer's directions and adding vegetables or fruit in accordance with pressure cooking timetable. Redevelop steam and continue to cook.
7. Flavors will be more pronounced in pressure cooked meals; therefore, reduce amounts of herbs and spices by one-fourth. For example, if your recipe calls for 1 teaspoon oregano, use 3/4 teaspoon oregano.
8. When cooking is complete, release pressure according to manufacturer's directions. Remove lid and stir well.
9. Taste and correct seasonings.
10. If the recipe seems to have too much liquid, cook over high heat, uncovered, to reduce excess liquid, stirring occasionally.

Herbs

Fresh Herbs
If there is a choice, select fresh herbs over dried. The flavor is pure, fresh, and pronounced.
  Store the fresh herbs by rinsing in cool water. Wrap stems in a damp paper towel and place them in a plastic bag or wrap loosely in plastic wrap.

Substituting Fresh for Dried Herbs
The rule for substituting fresh herbs in a recipe is to triple the amount specified. Example: 1 teaspoon dried dill = 3 teaspoons or 1 tablespoon fresh dill.

Herbs . . . A Lovely Touch to a Simple Recipe

Beef	Pork	Lamb	Veal/Poultry
Bay leaf	Allspice	Basil	Basil
Black peppercorns	Bay leaf	Bay leaf	Bay leaf
Cayenne	Cayenne	Curry	Cayenne
Cumin	Celery Seed	Dill-fennel	Chervil
Garlic	Cloves	Ginger	Marjoram
Marjoram	Curry powder	Marjoram	Fennel
Oregano	Ginger	Parsley	Oregano
Paprika	Oregano	Spearmint	Paprika
Rosemary	Parsley	Oregano	Rosemary
Red pepper flakes	Paprika	Red pepper flakes	Sage
Sage	Mustard (dried)	Rosemary	White pepper
Tarragon	Rosemary	Thyme	Tarragon
	Sage	Black pepper	Thyme
	Thyme		
	Black pepper		

Fish	Vegetables	Pasta/Rice
Basil	Basil	Basil
Bay leaf	Bay leaf	Dill
Cayenne	Chervil	Fennel
Celery seed	Dill	Marjoram
Chervil	Fennel	Oregano
Cilantro	Garlic	Saffron
Dill	Marjoram	Savory
Fennel	Oregano	White peppercorns
Oregano	Parsley	
Paprika	Red pepper flakes	
Savory	Rosemary	
Thyme	Tarragon	
White peppercorns	White peppercorns	

Bouquet garni: a delightful combination of herbs used to enhance the flavors of soups, stews, and sauces. In the summer, when fresh herbs are available, tie together, with cotton twine, 2 springs parsley, 1 sprig thyme, 1 sprig marjoram, and 1 bay leaf. Add to the ingredients while cooking your favorite dish.

  It's easy to keep dried bouquet garni on hand during winter months. Simply mix together in a jar 3 crumbled bay leaves, 1/4 cup dried parsley, 2 tablespoons thyme, and 2 tablespoons marjoram. Keep it stored in a pantry for future use. Make sure there is a tight lid on the jar.

Metric Conversion Chart

Comparison to Metric Measure

When You Know	Symbol	Multiply By	To Find	Symbol
teaspoons	tsp	5.0	milliliters	ml
tablespoons	tbsp	15.0	milliliters	ml
fluid ounces	fl. oz.	30.0	milliliters	ml
cups	c	0.24	liters	l
pints	pt.	0.47	liters	l
quarts	qt.	0.95	liters	l
ounces	oz.	28.0	grams	g
pounds	lb.	0.45	kilograms	kg
Fahrenheit	F	5/9 (after subtracting 32)	Celsius	C

Liquid Measure to Milliliters

1/4 teaspoon	=	1.25 milliliters
1/2 teaspoon	=	2.5 milliliters
3/4 teaspoon	=	3.75 milliliters
1 teaspoon	=	5.0 milliliters
1-1/4 teaspoons	=	6.25 milliliters
1-1/2 teaspoons	=	7.5 milliliters
1-3/4 teaspoons	=	8.75 milliliters
2 teaspoons	=	10.0 milliliters
1 tablespoon	=	15.0 milliliters
2 tablespoons	=	30.0 milliliters

Fahrenheit to Celsius

F	C
200–205	95
220–225	105
245–250	120
275	135
300–305	150
325–330	165
345–350	175
370–375	190
400–405	205
425–430	220
445–450	230
470–475	245
500	260

Liquid Measure to Liters

1/4 cup	=	0.06 liters
1/2 cup	=	0.12 liters
3/4 cup	=	0.18 liters
1 cup	=	0.24 liters
1-1/4 cups	=	0.3 liters
1-1/2 cups	=	0.36 liters
2 cups	=	0.48 liters
2-1/2 cups	=	0.6 liters
3 cups	=	0.72 liters
3-1/2 cups	=	0.84 liters
4 cups	=	0.96 liters
4-1/2 cups	=	1.08 liters
5 cups	=	1.2 liters
5-1/2 cups	=	1.32 liters

Index

Toula Patsalis is instructor of cooking and program director of four successful cooking schools affiliated with quality cookshops in the state of Michigan. She has studied cooking both in the U.S. and abroad. Toula is considered a culinary authority and has appeared regularly on television and various media talk shows.

Besides being a chairperson for cookbook projects to benefit the American Cancer Society and a local Greek Orthodox Cathedral, Toula Patsalis is a member of the International Association of Culinary Professionals and the American Institute of Wine and Food.

OTHER BOOKS OF INTEREST